W9-BXX-280

Spiritual Moments with the Great Composers

Daily Devotions from the Lives of Favorite Composers & Hymn Writers

Patrick Kavanaugh

Foreword by Jerome Hines, Metropolitan Opera

ZondervanPublishingHouse
Grand Rapids, Michigan

A Division of HarperCollins*Publishers*

Other books by Patrick Kavanaugh

The Spiritual Lives of Great Composers

A Taste for the Classics

Raising Musical Kids

To Elsie and Frank Beeler, my parents-in-law,
whose lives have inspired mine,
and who gave me my greatest gift,
their daughter Barbara

Spiritual Moments with the Great Composers

Requests for information should be addressed to:

 ZondervanPublishingHouse
Grand Rapids, Michigan 49530

Library of Congress Cataloging-in-Publication Data

Kavanaugh, Patrick.
Spiritual moments with the great composers : daily devotions from the lives of favorite composers and hymn writers / Patrick Kavanaugh.
p. cm.
Includes bibliographical references.
ISBN: 0-310-20042-3
1. Musicians—Prayer-books and devotions—English. 2. Church musicians—Prayer-books and devotions—English. 3. Devotional calendars. 4. Music—Religious aspects—Christianity—Meditations. 5. Composers. I. Title.
BV4596.M87K37 1995 95-23198
246'.7—dc20 CIP

This edition printed on acid-free paper and meets the American National Standards Institute Z39.48 standard.

Edited by Evelyn Bence
Interior design by Joe Vriend

Printed in the United States of America

95 96 97 98 99 00 01 02 /❖ DH / 10 9 8 7 6 5 4 3

Table of Contents

Foreword

Ever since King David wrote his many psalms, musicians of faith have attempted to serve God through the gifts He has given them. Often this service has been through direct service in the house of the Lord. The earliest patterns were given by the temple musicians, while today's examples include ministers of music as well as gospel music performers and composers.

But other Christian musicians have been called by God to serve in the secular arena. These include many of the world's greatest composers, who maintained their faith in Christ while daily working in the musical establishments of their day. Such men of history are paralleled in the hundreds of Christian singers and instrumentalists who serve in today's workforce of orchestras, opera companies, and music departments.

In this way, God has always preserved a light within the musical world through those who recognize that music was ultimately made to praise its Creator. In many ways, this call to be "in the world but not of it" is an enigmatic one for believers. The pressures put upon them are often so great as to make an effective witness for Christ very difficult.

For years since I gave my life to Jesus Christ, I have continued to work in the opera business, using the talents God has given me. Though it has not always been easy, many of my greatest joys were those times in which the Lord gave me the opportunity to bring forth a biblical response to a real world situation. Yet it is this very factor—the living out of a Christian life in a secular world—that gives us so much we can learn as we study the lives of the musicians featured in this book.

Dr. Patrick Kavanaugh has been examining our Christian musical heritage for many years. He is perhaps the perfect person to write such a "musical devotional," as he has spent his life both in full-time ministry and as a professional musician. Even before the

release of his book, *The Spiritual Lives of the Great Composers*, he was recognized as a leading authority in the study of Christian music.

I know Patrick to be more than a talented conductor and composer. He is a devout Christian whose love for the Lord shines through everything he does. We have performed together from Washington, D. C.'s Kennedy Center to Moscow's Bolshoi Theatre, and each concert began as we joined together in prayer for God's blessing. His work as the Executive Director of the Christian Performing Artists' Fellowship has inspired hundreds of Christian musicians to use their gifts for the glory of God.

I hope that as you read Patrick's stories, you too will be inspired to serve God with your gifts, whatever they may be. Let us "learn from those who have gone before" and receive God's grace so that we might "live a life worthy of the Gospel of Jesus Christ."

Jerome Hines

Jerome Hines
Metropolitan Opera

Introduction

Love of the Lord Jesus Christ and love of music—along with the love of my dear family—are *the* loves of my life. No competition. Each year, as I meet more and more Christian musicians and music lovers from all parts of the world, I find that many others share these two passions. Perhaps you do, as well.

As a younger man I loved music so much that I chose it as my profession. I earned several degrees in music (with studies in composition, theory, musicology, and conducting) and became a professional musician. A different course soon followed, as I was ordained and served on the pastoral staff of a church for several years. Finally, these two courses were united as I became the executive director of the Christian Performing Artists' Fellowship, a nationwide ministry dedicated to bringing the Gospel back into the world of the performing arts.

Over the years as I studied hundreds of great composers, I frequently noted how much we can learn from the life stories of these masters. As Christians we can grow as we emulate many of their virtues and as we heed the warnings evident in their mistakes.

My first efforts to bring together Christian principles and the world of music were biographical (*The Spiritual Lives of Great Composers,* published by Sparrow Press, 1991), musical (*A Taste for the Classics,* published by Sparrow Press, 1993), or educational (*Raising Musical Kids,* published by Servant Publications, 1995). Yet throughout my years of study and performance, a question has always held my attention: How can the love of music specifically help us become *closer to Christ?* Answering that question led to the writing of this book.

Certainly the inherent beauty of great music can itself draw us to Christ. I have heard many testimonies of people who, upon hearing a certain composition, were suddenly aware of their need for

God—a marvelous example of how music can be used to glorify the Lord.

But as I considered my own Christian walk, I knew that my daily quiet time—prayer, Bible study, and devotional reading—was the most important element in my relationship with Christ. The investment of time set apart for spiritual growth has reaped many wonderful dividends, and I write this devotional in the hope that it will enrich your daily quiet time—drawing you closer to God through the joy of music.

The concept is simple, and it is based on the premise that we want to learn something new every day and that we want to come closer to Christ every day. Devotional entries start with an experience in or characteristic of the life of a great composer, followed by a spiritual application for life today.

Most of the composers cited in this book we know to be professed Christians, but we can certainly learn from the experiences of all these musicians, whatever their backgrounds.

As you read these devotional selections, ask the Spirit to speak to you personally. I have written the stories not simply to amuse or educate, but also to inspire. Ask how each piece applies to your own situation.

In the seventy devotional pieces, I cover a wide spectrum of classical musicians and several hymnwriters. If I left out your favorite composer or anecdote, perhaps it can be included in a future edition. I know hundreds of other inspirational music stories.

As I finish this book, I echo the apostle Paul, who encouraged his fellow Christians with this prayer:

> May the Lord direct your hearts into God's love and Christ's perseverance (2 Thessalonians 3:5).

Patrick Kavanaugh
March 1995

Part One

Musical Encouragement

You Have the Power to Bless

But encourage one another daily,
as long as it is called Today.
Hebrews 3:13

Keep steadily on! I tell you,
you have the capability,
and do not let them intimidate you!
—Franz Liszt

Robert Schumann

ROBERT SCHUMANN (1810–1856)

Rare Recommendations

A man finds joy in giving an apt reply— and how good is a timely word!
—Proverbs 15:23

As a group, composers are not known for their praise of fellow composers. The temptation is to belittle the works of "competitors," trying to make one's own works look better by comparison. But Robert Schumann was a bright exception to this pattern.

As the editor of the publication *Neue Zeitschrift fur Musik*, his promotion of able composers often saved them from obscurity. Schumann considered his most important duty "to promote those younger talents." A few typical examples:

He called Mendelssohn "the Mozart of the nineteenth century, the most brilliant musician, the one who sees most clearly through the contradictions of this period, and for the first time reconciles them."

Concerning the almost unknown Schubert, he wrote, "It would require whole books to show in detail what works of pure genius his compositions are."

He considered Brahms "the one chosen to express the most exalted spirit of the times in an ideal manner."

Schumann especially praised Frédéric Chopin; a young man far from his native Poland, Chopin could easily have been ignored as a musical outsider. Yet when Schumann, carrying a Chopin score under his arm, entered a meeting of musicians, he proclaimed triumphantly, "Hats off, gentlemen—a genius!" Schumann wanted everyone to recognize

Chopin's talents, and he wrote that "Through him, Poland has obtained a seat and vote in the great musical parliament of the nations."

Of course these composers' names are now household words to us, but Schumann's recommendations and reviews often referred to complete unknowns. He repeatedly put his reputation on the line by publicly applauding the music of young, untested composers—and rather than advance his own music by degrading that of others, he freely extolled the efforts of his peers.

It is all too easy to criticize; it takes wisdom and discretion to find the good in others and name it publicly. Take a moment to consider: Do you know someone of whom you can speak positively today? A friend? Perhaps the son or daughter of a friend? Perhaps even someone who is not very popular and could use a good recommendation?

Ask God to bring someone in particular to your mind, remembering that "Pleasant words are a honeycomb, sweet to the soul and healing to the bones" (Prov. 16:24).

Father, I know that I have benefited from the good words others have spoken of me. I want to pass that blessing along to others. Help me today to discover in someone a good quality or a talent that I have previously overlooked. When I see it, help me to name it aloud. Give me words of recommendation to speak to those who need to hear them.

EDVARD GRIEG (1843–1907)

Blessing the Next Generation

Each generation of the upright will be blessed.
—Psalm 112:2

One of the most popular piano concertos is Edvard Grieg's *Concerto in A Minor.* From its dramatic opening to its electrifying finale, it stands alongside the *Peer Gynt Suite* as Grieg's most frequently performed composition.

This concerto and its composer got off to a good start owing to the encouragement of the greatest pianist of his time, Franz Liszt (1811–1886).

Soon after finishing the work, the youthful and jittery Grieg brought it to the renowned pianist. More than thirty years older than Grieg, the famed Liszt could be very intimidating. If he didn't like this piece, news would travel and the work might be doomed to obscurity.

Liszt welcomed the young composer by asking him to play the work himself. A flustered Grieg—he may have written the concerto, but he had never practiced it—answered simply, "I cannot."

With a reassuring smile, Liszt joked, "Very well, then I will show you that I also cannot." He then sight-read the entire work with incredible dexterity—to Grieg's utter delight.

As he played, Liszt made various bright remarks and nodded at significant sections. At one point he exploded with glee, then repeated the passage. After a triumphant conclusion, Liszt handed the manuscript back to Grieg saying,

"Keep steadily on! I tell you, you have the capability, and do not let them intimidate you!"

The young man never forgot those words of encouragement from such an established master and the day would come when an acclaimed Grieg would himself encourage younger composers. He later wrote, "This final admonition [of Liszt] was of tremendous importance to me. There was something in it that seemed to give it an air of sanctification."

Perhaps meeting young Grieg brought back an old memory to Franz Liszt: As a boy of twelve, he played the piano at a concert attended by the great Beethoven. Amid the applause, Beethoven rose, approached the stage, and kissed Franz's cheek as if in blessing—a blessing he could now pass on to some talented artisan much younger than he.

What young person have you blessed lately? One of the greatest needs of young people is that of affirmation, the "well-done" that comes when someone older and wiser says, "Great job" or "I'm really proud of you" or "You're going to make it."

Maybe your words can echo those of the Israelites to Ezra, "We will support you, so take courage and do it" (Ezra 10:4).

Maybe the blessing can be that of Franz Liszt: "Keep on! You have the capability, and don't let them intimidate you!"

Father, sometimes I'm so busy that I forget to notice the needs of others. Help me to slow down and take the time to encourage those around me. Bring a young person to mind and show me how to pray for him or her. Prompt me to encourage others whenever I have the chance. Let my words add a blessing to their lives.

Charlotte Elliott (1789–1871)

God Uses Each One of Us

Each one should use whatever gift he has received to serve others, faithfully administering God's grace in its various forms.
—1 Peter 4:10

The old woman wrestled with her indecision. She had been profoundly stirred by the preacher's message. She wanted to commit her life to Christ, but as she considered her frail body, her thoughts ran wild: *What would God want with me? God couldn't use me. I have nothing left to offer.*

Then the words of the choir overrode her depressive resistance: "Just as I am, without one plea." God wanted her now, in her fractured state. As this truth sunk in, the woman stood, along with many others, and made her way toward the front of the auditorium.

A century and a half earlier, in 1834, another woman had been similarly depressed. Charlotte Elliott was an invalid who lived with her family in Brighton, England. The house was a flurry of activity, helping her brother, a minister, as he organized a bazaar to raise money for the building of a nearby school. As the day approached, Charlotte became ill; she lay tossing on her bed, feeling miserable and utterly useless to the "cause" at hand.

That "helpless" situation turned a corner the next day. When the family had all left for the bazaar, God sent Charlotte a sudden awareness of great peace. In the quiet of the house she wrote the words that God would use to draw thousands to himself:

Just as I am, without one plea,
But that thy blood was shed for me,
And that thou bidd'st me come to thee,
O Lamb of God, I come.

Charlotte Elliott could never imagine how God would use those words in the coming decades. When she published the text in her *Invalid Prayer Book*, she inscribed this song with the words of Jesus, "Him that cometh to me I will in no wise cast out" (John 6:37 KJV).

Although Elliott's brother had an active, effective, public ministry, he admitted that his work seemed dwarfed in comparison to the ministry of his incapacitated sister: "In the course of a long ministry, I hope I have been permitted to see some of the fruit of my labor, but I feel that far more has been done by a single hymn of my sister's."

Even in our weakness, even when we are feeling "useless," we can be used by God to encourage others. God can take one small word of praise or effort of kindness for His glory and in a way that is beyond our imagination. It is like dropping a pebble into a pond and watching as the concentric waves disperse far and wide.

Just as you are, whom can you encourage today?

Father, help me to walk in Your strength and not my own. Forgive me for my self-pity when I feel "useless." Grant me faith to know that the small encouragements I give others will ripple on beyond the small sphere of my immediate world.

Pablo Casals (1876–1973)

Finding the Good to Praise

*Whatever is true,
whatever is noble,
whatever is right,
whatever is pure,
whatever is lovely,
whatever is
admirable—if
anything is excellent
or praiseworthy—
think about such
things.*
—Philippians 4:8

Pablo Casals, one of the greatest cellists of all time, revolutionized cello technique, thrilled millions of music lovers, moved dozens of composers to write works for his instrument, and composed for the cello himself. But his supreme contribution may be in the thousands of students he inspired.

Casals loved his students. In an age when critics were looking for one wrong note on which to condemn a young performer, Casals looked for the good in cellists under his tutelage.

An example was Gregor Piatigorsky (1903–1976), who would in time become one of the great cello master performers. As a young man, Piatigorsky was eager to play for the renowned Casals, but when the opportunity arrived, he unfortunately turned into a bundle of nerves. Botching every movement, he doggedly plowed through works of Bach, Beethoven, and Schumann—knowing he had disgraced himself.

But no. To Piatigorsky's amazement, at the end of the last piece Casals burst into applause and praise. He even leaned over and embraced the confused Piatigorsky, who knew that he had done poorly. How could this great man stoop to such patronizing praise?

In time, Piatigorsky's talents were evident to all, and as a fellow world-class performer, he developed a friendship with Casals. One night after the two had played duets for hours,

Piatigorsky mustered his courage and confronted Casals about that "undeserved praise" of long ago.

Casals hadn't forgotten the private performance, and he responded intensely: He quickly grabbed his cello and played a phrase from the very Beethoven sonata that Piatigorsky had blundered through. "Listen!" he shouted. "Didn't you play this fingering? It was novel to me . . . It was good . . . and here, didn't you attack that passage with up-bow, like this?" On and on he went, recalling the good in Piatigorsky's "inadequate" presentation.

He concluded with words that Piatigorsky never forgot: "And for the rest, leave it to the ignorant and stupid who judge by counting only the faults. I can be grateful, and so must you be, for even one note, one wonderful phrase."

Casals' words haunt me. How easy to see what's wrong rather than what's right or worthy of praise. Paul tells us to think about what is excellent, admirable, or praiseworthy. I suggest we take that a step further and talk about talents or actions or qualities that meet those qualifications.

Almost anyone can tell someone what he's doing wrong rather than what he's doing right. I do this all too often myself—with colleagues, with students, with my children, even with my wife. How much better life would be if I could learn the secret of Pablo Casals—the ability to inspire others by telling them the truth about what they do well.

Father, help me to see others as You see them, with eyes of love. Let me be grateful for even one good deed, one praiseworthy trait that I see in someone else. Use me to affirm the good in others.

FRANZ LISZT (1811–1886)

Praise Is Contagious

How beautiful on the mountains are the feet of those who bring good news.
—Isaiah 52:7

Today thousands of music lovers are devotees of Richard Wagner (1813–1883). Every year hundreds travel to Germany and pay the world's highest prices to attend the annual "Wagner's *Ring*" performances at Bayreuth Theatre, which Wagner built expressly for the huge twelve-hour production.

But Wagner's genius was not always recognized. His musical style was so advanced that many considered his work ludicrous. Only the finest musicians could understand Wagner's efforts, and most of them were busy with their own careers.

A notable exception was the pianist-composer Franz Liszt. Universally considered the greatest pianist of his age, Liszt was convinced of Wagner's genius and determined to spread the word.

For instance, one night Liszt particularly enjoyed an orchestra performance of the overture to Wagner's opera *Tannhauser.* But, from his box seat, he noted the audience's halfhearted applause at the end of the piece. Not content with such a response, he stood up, raised his hands above the crowd, and clapped thunderously. Recognizing the famous Liszt, the audience turned and enthusiastically cheered him. But Liszt turned the attention back to the stage, demanding that the music be played again. Following his lead, the crowd shouted for an encore; the orchestra repeated the overture, this time to a thunderous outburst of applause.

Another time Liszt heard in his native Hungary about an upcoming concert of Wagner's compositions in Budapest. Unsympathetic to the German Wagner and his music, the local press strongly discouraged attendance at the concert, and no one was buying tickets.

Fortunately, someone explained the situation to Liszt, who was deeply disappointed in his fellow Hungarians. Why couldn't they learn to appreciate Wagner's music? Quickly devising a plan, the crowd-pleasing virtuoso announced, "I will play Beethoven's *Concerto in E Flat Major* at the same concert." Within twenty-four hours the "Wagner concert" was sold out!

Eventually Liszt's "Wagner campaign" was successful, with more and more listeners tuning in to the complex music. Before he died, Liszt would hear critics claim that Wagner's compositional talents eclipsed his own. Rather than being envious of Wagner's ultimate success, Liszt was glad to see genius recognized and acclaimed.

Had it not been for this man's generous spirit, who knows whether Wagner's music would be performed today?

In the news these days, especially in election years, we hear often about "negative ad campaigns." The people who put those ads together know that criticism is contagious. But so is praise. When I hear a quality performance, see a good movie, discover a talented author, I like to spread the word: "You've got to check this out." In a way it's like being an evangelist trying to convert the skeptical to receive the Good News.

Why don't you join me in my positive ad campaign? Who knows? You might be responsible for turning an empty concert hall into a sell-out performance.

Father, give me a discerning eye to see value and virtue in what You deem valuable and virtuous. Give me the opportunity to spread the word and help influence the way people respond to what is worthy of acclaim.

Thomas Arne (1710–1778)

Opening Doors to Opportunity

And do not forget to do good and to share with others, for with such sacrifices God is pleased.
—Hebrews 13:16

The greatest British composer of the mid-eighteenth century was Thomas Arne, best known for his *Rule Britannia;* Wagner commented that the whole of English character is expressed in the first eight notes of this song.

As a boy, like Handel, Arne defied his father to study music, even secretly practicing his harpsichord by muffling the strings with a handkerchief.

As a man, he wrote for the London Theatre. His oratorio *Judith* featured the first woman ever to sing in a British chorus. Arne was best known for his operas, including *Artaxerxes,* a great favorite of Haydn.

What motivated Arne's works? While many of his contemporaries went for bottom-line profits, Arne created with a more personal—and person-centered—agenda. Living in an age when a composer could choose his own star performers, Arne composed the huge opera *Rosamond* with his sister in mind. When it opened, she stepped onto the stage in the leading role, launching an operatic career. Later, he wrote the opera *Tom Thumb* so his little brother could play the heroic role.

In such endeavors Arne worked for months with the goal of furthering the career of those he loved. Already celebrated for his talent, he could have chosen any soloists in England, and some "stars" might well have enhanced his

own interests. Yet he chose to use his talents to open opportunities for others.

Perhaps you have achieved a certain level of success in your profession. You may already have tasted the joy of using that success to bless others less experienced than yourself. If so, you'll need little prodding to continue using your gifts to encourage others. If not, why not try to experiment? Think of a way to open a door of opportunity for someone else. It might take time. It might mean mentoring and coaching, but the satisfaction of seeing someone blossom is greater than any amount of money or fame can supply.

Father, You have never been stingy with me. First, You have given me gifts and talents, and then You have given me the opportunity to develop them. Let me pass on the blessing to someone else who needs an open door of opportunity.

Frédéric Chopin (1810–1849)

Rooted and Inspired

I pray that you, being rooted and established in love, may have power, together with all the saints, to grasp how wide and long and high and deep is the love of Christ, and to know this love that surpasses knowledge.
—Ephesians 3:17–19

It is hard to separate the music or life story of Frédéric Chopin from his native, war-torn Poland. While living in Vienna, he heard that Russia had captured Warsaw, and he composed a protest piece called *Revolutionary Etude*. After disasters in Poland, he wrote his famous *Funeral March*. A century later, when the Nazis invaded in 1939, Chopin's music became a national rallying cry. Before Warsaw's surrender, the last music played on the radio was Chopin's *Polonaise in A Major.*

Chopin's personal patriotism was rooted in his deep affection for his loving, supportive family. His parents praised his musical efforts and sacrificed to find him the best teachers available. When he left Poland in 1830, his mother's last words spoke of her confident belief in her son: "Frédéric, thou wilt be a great musician. Thy Poland will be proud of thee."

His principal teacher, Warsaw composer Joseph Elsner, was equally inspiring, quickly recognizing Chopin's extraordinary gifts and aiding him in every way without a hint of rivalry or envy of his student's greater talent. Elsner loved to repeat a favorite maxim: "It is not enough for a student to equal or surpass his master; he should create an individuality of his own." That's a laudatory attitude, considering the fact that too many teachers of the creative arts insist that their students imitate their own styles and not grow beyond a prescribed "box."

Chopin's parents and teachers took great pride in his accomplishments, seeing him blossom into Poland's greatest musical son. And Chopin knew the value of the good-faith gifts they had given him. When the twenty-year-old pianist left Poland to seek his fortune, Joseph Elsner gave him a silver urn filled with the soil of his native land. To his dying day, Chopin packed that silver urn in his travel bags, and even then . . . well, it was buried with him when he died prematurely in Paris at the age of thirty-nine, in 1849.

Frédéric Chopin carried a heartful of encouraging memories that rooted him—even as he traveled far from home—and inspired an amazingly productive though short life.

Maybe you were similarly inspired by someone who believed in you at a critical time. Look around your home or office. Do you value certain mementos that speak a clear message that you are rooted and encouraged by loved ones who live far away?

Stop and thank God for these people who have encouraged you over the years—by their prayers, their cards, and calls. Why not even call one of your "supporters" today—just to say "thanks for rooting me"?

Father, I have learned something about Your love for me as I have received the encouraging love of a few special brothers and sisters. Thank You for their presence in my life.

Part Two

MUSICAL JOY

The Gift of a Cheerful Heart

This is the day the LORD has made;
let us rejoice and be glad in it.
Psalm 118:24

Since God has given me a cheerful heart,
he will forgive me for serving him cheerfully.
—Franz Joseph Haydn

Johann Sebastian Bach and Family

Johann Sebastian Bach (1685–1750)

Joy in God's Presence

The trumpeters and singers joined in unison, as with one voice, to give praise and thanks to the Lord. Accompanied by trumpets, cymbals and other instruments, they raised their voices in praise to the Lord and sang: "He is good; his love endures forever." Then the temple of the Lord was filled with a cloud, and the priests could not perform their service because of the cloud, for the glory of the Lord filled the temple of God.

—2 Chronicles 5:13–14

This Old Testament Scripture from 2 Chronicles describes a worship service the day the ark of the covenant was brought into Solomon's splendid new temple in Jerusalem.

Next to these verses, in the margin of his biblical commentary, Johann Sebastian Bach wrote: "Where there is devotional music, God is always at hand with His gracious presence."

Johann Sebastian Bach was a career church musician in Germany. He often practiced and worked in the church itself—basking in the joy of God's presence.

Even two centuries after the Reformation, Martin Luther's influence permeated the country. Luther had revolutionized faith—and music; he had declared music to be second only to the Gospel itself.

As for Bach, a Luther disciple, he claimed that "Music's only purpose should be for the glory of God and the recreation of the human spirit."

Bach worked as if God were at his shoulder, directing the scene. When staring at a page he needed to fill with notes—to have a new composition ready for the Sunday service, he often initialed the blank manuscript with "J. J.," which stood for *Jesu Juva,* meaning "Help me, Jesus." After finishing a manuscript, he frequently initialed the last page with "S. D. G.," denoting

Soli Deo Gloria or "To God Alone the Glory." The composer was ever aware of God's being with him, guiding his work.

When it came to his awareness of God, Bach made little distinction between sacred and secular music. At the beginning of his "secular" *Little Organ Book,* he wrote: "To God alone the praise be given for what's herein to man's use written." His *Little Clavier Book* was inscribed "In the Name of Jesus."

Bach's son Carl Philipp Emanuel noted that the whole Bach family "were in the habit of beginning all things with religion."

Not every Christian is called to full-time church work as Bach was for most of his life. We may not spend our days practicing a church organ or for a church performance. But all of us can be constantly aware of God's presence at our shoulder, by our side, even in our spirits.

As I go about my work today, I pray for joy that will fill my mind with music—a heavenly music even more magnificent than any the great Bach ever wrote on a blank manuscript page.

Father, help me to be aware of Your presence every day, no matter what my circumstances or environment—as I work or play, as I worship in a church building dedicated to You, as I walk amid Your creation, and through the artistic creations—music, poetry, art—that bring glory to Your name.

LUDWIG VAN BEETHOVEN (1770–1827)

An Ode to Joy Amid the Silence

Those who sow in tears will reap with songs of joy.
—Psalm 126:5

Brothers, o'er yon
starry sphere,
Sure there dwells a
loving Father,
O ye millions, kneel
before Him,
World, dost feel thy
Maker near?
Seek Him o'er yon
starry sphere,
O'er the stars
enthroned, adore
Him!

—from Friedrich von Schiller's "Ode to Joy," used by Beethoven in the final movement of his Symphony no. 9

For many decades if you asked musicians to name the world's greatest symphony, most would have answered, "the Ninth!" They would be referring, of course, to Ludwig van Beethoven's last—his Symphony no. 9 in D Minor.

Every movement is a masterpiece, and its novel finale adds a large chorus to the immense orchestra. Audiences and performers alike revere the Ninth. Hundreds of orchestras have recorded it, and thousands of students have scrutinized its magnificent pages. The work exudes such ecstasy and joy that the last movement's principal theme is sung in many churches as a hymn of praise to God: "Joyful, Joyful, We Adore Thee."

Ironically, Beethoven wrote this composition in one of the saddest periods of his life. His hearing loss was dramatic. He could no longer perform as a virtuoso pianist. Although he was known as a great symphonist, it would be ten long years (1814–1824) between the premieres of his Eighth Symphony and his Ninth.

In this decade several of his closest friends and patrons died (Prince Kinsky, Prince Carl Lichnowsky, and Prince Lobowitz), leaving Beethoven with fewer benefactors and a reduced income. Lamentably, another close friendship, with Stephen Breuning, was dissolved after a heated argument. Yet

another friend, Johann Nepomuk Maelzel, stole a "Battle-Piece" (celebrating Wellington's Waterloo victory over Napoleon) Beethoven had composed for him, resulting in painful lawsuits. Finally, Beethoven's brother died, leaving the bachelor composer feeling a misguided obligation to take care of his eight-year-old nephew, Carl—to the misery of everyone involved.

In midst of these misfortunes, Beethoven's diary revealed that he turned more and more to God to find inner joy. The wretched composer cried out, "God, help me! Thou seest me deserted by all mankind. I do not want to do wrong—hear my prayer to be with my Carl for the future for which there seems to be no possibility now." Another diary entry reads, "O God, give me the strength to overcome myself; nothing must hold me to this life." He wrote to a friend in 1821, "God, who knows my innermost soul, and knows how sacredly I have fulfilled all the duties put upon me as man by humanity, God, and nature, will surely someday relieve me from these afflictions."

At long last, the Ninth Symphony was finished. He'd heard the chords and chorus only in his mind. How would the world respond? Would this piece be discounted as the work of an old, crazed man?

At the final note of the premiere, the audience exploded with thunderous applause. But the composer, standing next to the conductor with his back to the crowd, looked straight ahead, hearing nothing. Fortunately, the solo contralto noticed Beethoven's disorientation and turned him around so he could see and take a bow before the cheering crowd. *Joy!*

In the midst of a painful situation, it is difficult to find any joy. But Jesus, at the Last Supper, gave his disciples hope for inner peace and joy that would carry them through dark

times: "I have told you these things, so that *in me* you may have peace. In this world you will have trouble. But take heart! I have overcome the world" (John 16:33 [italics added]).

In Christ we are overcomers, singing an ode to the Overcomer who brings us joy.

Father, sometimes the pain of life seems overwhelming. Please keep me close to You in these times and help me to find joy and peace in the midst of the storm. Jesus, in You I have peace.

Blessed are those who have learned to acclaim you, who walk in the light of your presence, O LORD. *They rejoice in your name all day long; they exult in your righteousness.*
—Psalm 89:15–16

FRANZ JOSEPH HAYDN (1732–1809)

Never Let Go of Joy

The life of Austrian composer Franz Joseph Haydn might be summarized by another Old Testament line: "The joy of the LORD is your strength" (Neh. 8:10).

His joyful attitude was not the result of a life free of obstacles. He was born in poverty, had a difficult marriage, and worked hard to make a living, yet he never let trying circumstances darken his enthusiastic nature or weaken his faith.

Haydn's exuberant compositions reflect his cheerful temperament. His music was so buoyant that it was once criticized by his church. How did the composer respond? "Since God has given me a cheerful heart, He will forgive me for serving him cheerfully." When Haydn considered the love of God, he said his heart "leapt for joy."

Remembering former struggles with the composition of a certain sacred work, Haydn wrote, "I prayed to God—not like a miserable sinner in despair—but calmly, slowly. In this I felt that an infinite God would surely have mercy on His finite creature, pardoning dust for being dust. These thoughts cheered me up. I experienced a sure joy so confident that as I wished to express the words of the prayer, I could not express my joy, but gave vent to my happy spirits and wrote 'Allegro' above the *Miserere* [Have Mercy]. "

Another time, sitting at his piano, setting to music the familiar Latin text *Agnus Dei, qui tollis peccata mundi* ("Lamb of God, who takes away the sins of the world"), he was suddenly compelled to scribble musical notes across his paper, the result of an "uncontrollable gladness." Throughout the centuries, composers had given this solemn text solemn music. That was not what came from Haydn's pen. Later, after this music was performed, he again felt compelled—this time to apologize lest he might have offended the listening Empress Marie Therese; he explained that the knowledge of God's grace had given him such happiness that he had written a cheerful melody to accompany sober words.

Haydn held fast to the joy of the Lord, even to the end of his seventy-seven years. In his last days he peacefully told a friend, "I have only to wait like a child for the time when God calls me to himself."

Whether or not God grants me or you a long life, I pray that He would grace us, His sons and daughters, with what I call a Haydn outlook—the ability to see this life and the next through the eyes of a joyful child.

Father, You know me completely. You know how quickly my mood can change from joy to frustration and anxiety. Give me the gift You gave to Your servant Haydn: the gift of a cheerful heart, so that even in trial and to my dying day I may relish the joy of Your presence.

Let us fix our eyes on Jesus, the author and perfecter of our faith, who for the joy set before him endured the cross, scorning its shame, and sat down at the right hand of the throne of God.
—Hebrews 12:2

Bernard of Clairvaux (1090–1153)

For the Joy Set Before Him

For almost nine centuries, one particular hymn has come to exemplify the passion of Jesus Christ. In America, it is known as "O Sacred Head, Now Wounded." It is sung to a melody used by many composers through the centuries, notably Johann Sebastian Bach in his *Saint Matthew's Passion*. The hymn poignantly depicts our Lord in His suffering and expresses our own anguish on seeing Christ scourged and slain for our sins.

O Sacred Head, now wounded,
With grief and shame weighed down,
Now scornfully surrounded
With thorns, thine only crown;

How pale thou art with anguish,
With sore abuse and scorn!
How does that visage languish
Which once was bright as morn!

The man who wrote the text to this moving hymn also knew weakness and scorn. Bernard of Clairvaux was born in Fontaines, France, around the year 1090. No one expected much of this frail child, who in time was deemed too weak to serve in the military.

Devoted to his Lord, the young man entered a monastery. Here, he might have buried himself along with thousands of other young monks in the Middle Ages, never to be remem-

bered in the annals of history. But God had a great task for this weak boy.

In the monastery, Bernard's superiors noticed his enthusiasm and ability to motivate his fellow monks into greater love of Jesus. Within three years of his arrival, Bernard was sent out to found and ordain the new monastery of Clairvaux. Could this weakling possibly succeed in such a daunting task?

With zeal and faith as his primary resources, Bernard launched the enterprise. His spirited preaching proved popular among the country people. Before long, dozens of men came knocking on his door, committing their lives to the service of Christ. The Clairvaux monastery, of which Bernard was abbot until his death in 1153, became well-known throughout all of Christendom as a bastion of Christian faith and ministry.

Bernard daily exhorted his men to live "in a manner worthy of the gospel of Christ" (Phil. 1:27). Outside the monastery, he preached the gospel to the rich and the poor, to well-educated scholars and rural farmers. He wrote many tracts and songs and personally helped found more than five hundred other monasteries.

How can this be, that such a hopeless failure with little promise became God's messenger to an entire generation? There were surely young men nearby with more talent, more education, more of a "future." Yet Bernard had something that most of his contemporaries lacked: an unquenchable love for God and an enthusiasm that motivated his own service and the service of others. This was the key to his monastery, his life, and his powerful ministry.

The frail-framed Bernard of Clairvaux is now seen as the most significant spiritual leader of his century. To me, his life is a reflection of the passion he described so poignantly in the

great hymn. The passion of Christ is further explained in Hebrews 12:2 in the context of joy: "For the joy set before him" he endured and then was given his heavenly reward "at the right hand of the throne of God."

The apostle Peter gives more insight into the joy we can know in the Lord because Christ endured through His passion and rose from the dark grave: "Though you have not seen him, you love him; and even though you do not see him now, you believe in him and are filled with an inexpressible and glorious joy" (1 Peter 1:8).

Notice that Peter did not write that we would *someday* be filled with this joy, once all our sufferings have ended. He states that we *are* filled with an inexpressible and glorious joy—no matter what our circumstances.

Do you feel weak today? Rather than focus on your weakness, fix your eyes on Jesus and go for the joy and His enduring strength.

Jesus, you took the sufferings of the world upon Yourself so that I can know Your joy—here and now. Thank You and help me to rely on Your strength when I feel frail.

Felix Mendelssohn-Bartholdy (1809–1847)

Expect Success

"For I know the plans I have for you," declares the Lord, "plans to prosper you and not to harm you, plans to give you hope and a future."
—Jeremiah 29:11

"Felix" in Latin means "happy man." What an appropriate name for this master composer, Felix Mendelssohn-Bartholdy. It would seem that God had picked out this name specifically for this man, and perhaps Mendelssohn considered his name a prophetic gift. This composer chose to ignore the possibility of failure, always expecting that eventually success would be granted.

Although he had his share of misfortunes, Mendelssohn, an optimistic man of strong Christian faith, was always quick to pull out of them and prevail. He seemed to move from victory to victory in his musical career.

Mendelssohn expected the best from life and usually received it. Let's look at a few of his accomplishments—the result of God's blessing on his great hope:

As a teenager, Mendelssohn set his heart on being a great musician—and he was. When he "found" and promoted the long-ignored music of J. S. Bach, he expected everyone to share his enthusiasm. And they did. One of his desires was to create a great music school. He opened the doors of the renowned Leipzig Conservatory of Music in 1843, and it has since schooled many of Europe's finest musicians. He anticipated becoming the conductor of a major orchestra, and he was granted the podium of Leipzig's prestigious Gewandhaus Orchestra.

His positive expectations extended beyond his musicianship and into his personal life. He enjoyed a wealth of fine friends, including some of the greatest composers of his day. And, yes, Mendelssohn was blessed with a wonderful, loving marriage. His relationship to his beloved Cecile was marked with passion, romance, and enduring love.

This "success" story doesn't discount trials or years of hard work. His own teacher had little faith in Mendelssohn's Bach revival. He faced many obstacles with the Conservatory, dealing with a king who was reluctant to grant needed permission and funds. He had to persevere through a wretched conducting season in Dusseldorf before he received the Gewandhaus post, but through his struggles he always expected success.

In Jesus' Prodigal Son story, the father figure is usually tied to the role of God—eagerly awaiting a wandering child's homecoming. But each of us can learn a lesson from that father—and from Mendelssohn—to expect the best.

Of the Roman Christians, Paul asked, "If God is for us, who can be against us?" (Rom. 8:31). That's the spirit that expects success.

Father, thank You for having great expectations of me. Give me faith to believe You for the fulfillment of those great things. Give me the confident joy that knows that "I can do everything through him who gives me strength" (Phil. 4:13).

Martin Rinkart (1586–1649)

Gratitude in Dark Times

Give thanks in all circumstances, for this is God's will for you in Christ Jesus.
—1 Thessalonians 5:18

Martin Rinkart wanted to weep. How many more funerals would he need to perform before the greedy jaws of war and plague would finally close? He had just finished preaching over the body of today's fiftieth victim. Little did he know that he would bury 4,400 people in his town of Eilenburg in Saxony before year's end.

Rinkart was the only clergyman in a city flooded with refugees from the Thirty-Years' War. Wherever he looked, the victims of hunger, poverty, and bloodshed were strewn like rotting flowers across the city streets. To make matters worse, the devastating pestilence of 1637 had swept through the city, claiming hundreds as its prey—among them Rinkart's wife.

If any man's cup of suffering was overflowing, it was Rinkart's. Yet the sorrow he endured never eclipsed his faith and hope. Instead, he used these dark years of his ministry to write a hymn that has sparked hope in hearts for more than three centuries.

Now thank we all our God
With heart and hands and voices,
Who wondrous things hath done,
In whom this world rejoices.
Who, from our mother's arms
Hath blest us on our way
With countless gifts of love
And still is ours today.

With the world unraveling around him, Rinkart refused to bow to despair. Instead, he praised God, thanking him for the "countless gifts of love" and the "wondrous things" He had done.

Martin Rinkart lived to see the end of the Thirty Years' War. When the Peace of Westphalia was concluded, the hymn sung in celebration was none other than Rinkart's "Now Thank We All Our God." The tune, composed by Rinkart's contemporary, Johann Cruger (1598–1662), has been borrowed by composers from Bach to Mendelssohn. Even now its strains seem to embody the essence of Christian gratitude and praise.

Few of us have known the prolonged, sharp-edged suffering that Rinkart endured, but all of us have experienced times of grief, rejection, and pain from which we thought we might never emerge. How can we possibly experience the gratitude and hope evident in Rinkart's words?

Fortunately, Martin Rinkart's secret is still available to us, and it is rooted in relationship with Christ. I challenge you today to praise God for His countless gifts of love—even if you don't *feel* that love. As Paul exhorted the Philippian believers: "Rejoice in the Lord always" (Phil. 4:4).

Over the years I've learned that as I praise God, I feel joy. As I praise, my vision is lifted beyond my current shortsightedness. As I praise, my spirit is lifted so that I feel the love of God, who is Love.

Father, I choose to lift my eyes to You and praise You for who You are. I may not feel overwhelmed by specific evidence of Your love, and yet I can identify and thank You for one particular "gift": ____________. With Rinkart and with the apostle Paul, I rejoice and thank You and claim the joy of the Spirit.

Wolfgang Amadeus Mozart (1756–1791)

Blessing Beyond Myself

May the God of hope fill you with all joy and peace as you trust in him, so that you may overflow with hope by the power of the Holy Spirit.
—Romans 15:13

The joyful Franz Joseph Haydn had a younger friend who also had a gift for a childlike joy—Wolfgang Amadeus Mozart—who exhibited an enthusiasm for life that fueled an amazingly fruitful productivity, often in the midst of great poverty and adversity.

Like the apostle Paul, Mozart had to learn "the secret of being content in any and every situation, whether well fed or hungry, whether living in plenty or in want" (Phil. 4:12). Mozart leaves us no "rags to riches" story—just the opposite. For this master the riches turned to rags.

Mozart's childhood acclaim is legendary. By age six he was touring and performing before European nobility. By his death at age thirty-five, he was barely staving off poverty. What happened? Whole books could be written answering the question. Mozart had little sense of fiscal responsibility. He was generous, some would say, to a fault. Harsh and envious critics tried to undermine him. And, maybe most influential—a fickle audience grew indifferent once the child prodigy, such a novelty, grew up.

Yet in the worst of times, Mozart never succumbed to a paralyzing depression. In fact, adversity seemed to inspire him to work. When pressured by financial disasters, Mozart would immediately begin a new composition. When he saw other composers receiving honors and denouncing his best efforts,

he would create innovative compositions that would someday triumph over the trite melodies of his competitors.

Mozart had the wonderful virtue of refusing to allow circumstances to affect his musical output. Even when he didn't have specific commissions, he composed—seemingly for the pure joy of it.

Four years before his untimely death, a frail Mozart was aware of his mortality. He wrote, "I never lie down in my bed without reflecting that perhaps I—young as I am—may not live to see another day; yet none of all who know me can say that I am socially melancholy or morose. For this blessing I daily thank my Creator and wish it from my heart for all my fellow men."

Recent film caricatures would have us believe that Mozart was a debauched man with little spiritual sensitivity. Though there are contradictions in his complex character, these lines thanking God for the blessing of a light spirit give a more accurate portrayal of a man with a deep Christian faith:

"For this blessing I daily thank my Creator and wish it from my heart for all my fellow men." What does he wish for others? The blessing of a cheerful and hopeful attitude, even in the face of frail health or poverty or an uncertain future.

It is also at the heart of the prayer that Paul made for the Christians in Rome: "May the God of hope fill you with all joy and peace as you trust in him, so that you may overflow with hope by the power of the Holy Spirit" (Rom. 15:13).

And it is the blessing we can pray for ourselves *and also* for our families, friends, and colleagues—all the fellow mortals who accompany us on our journeys.

Father, I pray that You would bless my home, my workplace, my world with a joyous spirit that remains even when circumstances fluctuate. Help me to be an instrument of that joy, sharing the peace and blessing of Christ with all who cross my path.

Part Three

Musical Excellence

The Beauty of Giving Your All

Whatever you do, work at it with all your heart,
as working for the Lord, not for men,
since you know that you will receive an inheritance from the Lord
as a reward. It is the Lord Christ you are serving.
Colossians 3:23–24

I know perfectly well that no musician can make his thoughts or his talents different from what Heaven has made them; but I also know that if Heaven had given him good ones, he must also be able to develop them properly.
—Felix Mendelssohn-Bartholdy

Felix Mendelssohn-Bartholdy

Felix Mendelssohn-Bartholdy (1809–1847)

Getting Down to the Details

From everyone who has been given much, much will be demanded; and from the one who has been entrusted with much, much more will be asked.
—Luke 12:48

Felix Mendelssohn's oratorio *Saint Paul* is one of history's finest musical biographies, and the story of Paul's conversion to Christ must have been very close to the heart of this composer—a Jewish convert himself.

Mendelssohn, always a meticulous worker, seemed to have taken particular pains with this composition. In one letter he refers to this oratorio and says, "I must not make any mistakes." To "get it right," he read everything he could on Greek and church history and on first-century life in Palestine.

This determination for excellence is part of what made Mendelssohn a master composer. Throughout the ages, lesser men, perhaps with the same intellect but without this conviction, have composed music. But its lack of flawlessness resulted in eventual oblivion. The impeccable minutia of a master's work gives the world something that will endure the test of time.

This is not to discount Mendelssohn's natural talent as a piano prodigy and a mental genius. One day a friend interrupted Mendelssohn when the composer was writing music. The friend started to leave, but Mendelssohn invited him to stay and converse, saying, "I am merely copying out." The friend was puzzled; there were no evident notes being copied. Mendelssohn was obviously composing, but he saw it as

simply writing down something he already had "finished" in his mind. The results? His Grand Overture in C Major.

Mendelssohn's genius and his wealthy background could have easily encouraged a disinterested attitude toward work. Not so. His composing career was based on a firm belief in divine inspiration and a Protestant work ethic: "I know perfectly well that no musician can make his thoughts or his talents different to [*sic*] what Heaven has made them; but I also know that if Heaven had given him good ones, he must also be able to develop them properly."

"To develop them properly" might have been Mendelssohn's life motto. Every year he strove to improve his own talents. Every performance found him giving his maximum, and in every composition, he worked out the smallest detail to perfection.

Sometimes I sense that we Christians rely so much on a principle of grace and forgiveness that we forget about biblical injunctions to strive for excellence.

Some people seem temperamentally better able than others to tend to "every detail." You may be one of those who prefers to deal with the "broad strokes" of life, yet I challenge you to reach for Mendelssohn's standards—taking healthy pride in doing a job worthy of the word *masterpiece.*

Consider the wisdom of Solomon: "Do you see a man skilled in his work? He will serve before kings; he will not serve before obscure men" (Proverbs 22:29).

Lord, forgive my sloppy habits and dismal excuses. Help me to see excellence with new commitment and to purpose to give You only my finest efforts. Lord, help me to see my work for others as work provided for You.

ANTONIO STRADIVARIUS (1644–1737)

Excellence—A Team Effort

But we have this treasure in jars of clay to show that this all-surpassing power is from God and not from us.
—2 Corinthians 4:7

I smile when I read these lines from a George Eliot poem titled "Stradivarius":

'Tis God gives skill,
But not without men's hands:
He could not make
Antonio Stradivari's violins
Without Antonio.

The great Antonio Stradivarius was the world's most celebrated maker of stringed instruments—violins, violas, cellos, and basses.

Long before names such as Rolls Royce or Hilton bespoke quality, Stradivarius was a synonym for superior craftsmanship. Even now "a Stradivarius" is a descriptive noun describing an excellent product. A sales rep might refer to "the Stradivarius of new cars" or "the Stradivarius of personal computers."

Antonio shared his secrets with his two sons and partners, Francesco (1671–1743) and Omobono (1679–1742). Though their "magic" was buried with them, the results of their work live on; many of their instruments are still played today—archetypes of craftsmanship and excellence. After three centuries, they are sold for hundreds of thousands—even millions!—of dollars.

Antonio's life work is seen in three distinct parts: From 1668 to 1686—for twenty years—he experimented to find the best woods for his instruments; he later destroyed many of these because they did not meet with his high standards. In the second period, from 1686 to 1694, he constructed somewhat larger instruments with substantially improved tone. Then from 1694 until his death in 1737, this Italian master reached a perfection in his art never to be surpassed—even by his trained sons.

His instruments were "without fault or blemish"—as close to perfection as humans can attain. And what's even more amazing, Antonio didn't dawdle over his task. He averaged finishing one violin per week!

What is it that makes a Stradivarius violin so magnificent? What was the great secret that hundreds of experts have tried unsuccessfully to copy?

Entire books, some including the most precise technical details, have been written on this subject. Whatever scientific answers there may be, all the experts agree on the extraordinary amount of *care* that went into each instrument. No sloppiness, no careless corner cutting—ever.

It's a standard of quality that is nearly too high to aim for. *I can't be perfect,* you might say, *so why should I even try to "go for the gold medal"?*

Instead of getting depressed and disheartened, go back and read again the lighthearted lines in the George Eliot poem and ask yourself one question: *Does God need me and my best effort to carry out His most excellent work?*

Throughout history God has chosen to use mortal men and women—"jars of clay"—to do His perfect work. He made Antonio's hands—and yours. What excellent work does He ask you to do with them—today?

Lord, You and I can team up to be partners on a winning team. I want to give You—and my fellow men and women—my best shot. Thanks for being with me in this venture.

Peter Illych Tchaikovsky (1840–1893)

Going the Extra Mile

If someone forces you to go one mile, go with him two miles.
—Matthew 5:41

As a young student at the Conservatory in Saint Petersburg, Peter Illych Tchaikovsky was named among the gifted and talented.

After hearing Tchaikovsky's early cantata, "Ode to Joy," Hermann Laroche (who would become one of Russia's most important music critics) said to him, "You are the greatest musical talent of contemporary Russia . . . In you I see the greatest, or rather the only, hope of our musical future."

Why did the young Tchaikovsky inspire such assertions? It was not mere natural talent. He also exhibited a consistent desire to give more than was required—to "go the extra mile." This was a trademark he would carry throughout his long and productive career.

One day his conservatory teacher, Nikolay Rubinstein, gave his composition class an assignment to write out contrapuntal variations on a given theme. The project was designed to force the students to produce quantity as well as quality. Emphasizing that he wanted the students to bring back as many variations as possible, Rubinstein expected Tchaikovsky and the other young musicians to write about a dozen each.

At the next class, Tchaikovsky nonchalantly handed in more than two hundred variations! Indeed, for this student such productivity became the standard. Testifying to the

quality and intricacy of each variation that Tchaikovsky turned in that day, an amazed Rubinstein noted, "To examine all these would have taken me more time than it took him to write them."

A teacher who finds a talented student with such determination to excel can sense a master in the making. Those students who do *more* than is required step out from the crowd. They're the ones who "win the race."

Today, once or twice ask yourself, "What is expected of me in this task? How can I go beyond these expectations? What will it take for me to do my very best even if best isn't required?"

Go for it—for the sheer pleasure of knowing that you've done your best. After all, "The desires of the diligent are fully satisfied" (Prov. 13:4).

Lord, help me to "go the extra mile" and do more than is expected of me. Forgive me when I settle for minimum efforts, or hold back when I could give more. Thank You for the diligent example of Tchaikovsky, and I pray that the same diligence might be found in my life, to Your great glory.

Carl Czerny (1791–1857)

Redeeming the Time

As long as it is day, we must do the work of him who sent me. Night is coming, when no one can work.
—John 9:4

As you read this, a piano student sits somewhere in a small practice room, doggedly working through "Czerny exercises." If you've ever taken piano lessons yourself, you might groan when you see Czerny's name. Generations of pianists have warmed up each day by playing a regimen of keyboard calisthenics composed by the Austrian Carl Czerny.

Although he wrote large concertos and sonatas, he is remembered best for his piano etudes, many with forbidding names such as *Die Schule der Gelaufigkeit* or *The School of Velocity*. (As a notable aside, he linked two pianistic ages: He studied with Beethoven and later taught Franz Liszt.)

Who was this man who has challenged piano students for more than a century? In his day he was a legend of resourcefulness; he knew something about time management long before it was a field for high-priced consultants. He composed hundreds of pieces, was one of Europe's best music editors—publishing the world's first complete edition of the keyboard music of J. S. Bach—and he never employed a copyist, meaning that he wrote every note himself.

Czerny fascinated his visitors by the unique practice of working at several tasks simultaneously, determined to use *all* his time productively. An English musician once reported on the four desks, one in each corner of Czerny's study:

The first desk contained a long list of national tunes to be arranged for D'Almaine and Co. At the second, there was an unfinished arrangement of Beethoven Symphonies (piano, four hands) for Cocks and Co. The third desk contained his new edition of Bach fugues, and at the fourth was a Grand Symphony Czerny was composing.

What a picture of creative productivity! Here is a man who knew how to redeem the hours in his day to ensure optimum production. And his work is still being appreciated (or at least tolerated!) by students today as they practice to achieve higher degrees of excellence.

From time to time we should examine how we spend the hours of any given day. One of the best witnesses to our society can be the testimony of the person known for productivity as well as quality in craftsmanship—the person who redeems the time at hand.

Father, help me to make good use of the hours in this day. Help me to be productive in a way that counts for eternity and in a way that proclaims a silent witness to Your excellent ways.

Leonard Bernstein (1918–1990)

Prepared for Any Opportunity

Be prepared in season and out of season.
—2 Timothy 4:2

I'm afraid I wasn't yet "part of the scene," but I'm told that in 1943, millions of war-weary, music-minded Americans eagerly anticipated radio broadcasts of the New York Philharmonic. On Sunday afternoon, November 14, the concert was to have been conducted by the eminent Bruno Walter, but on Saturday the maestro had fallen ill—too sick to "go on." Artur Rodzinski, the orchestra's music director, was snowbound in Massachusetts. His answer to the problem: "Call Bernstein."

Who? Leonard Bernstein was the newly appointed assistant conductor. Though obviously talented, he was young—twenty-five. He'd conducted rehearsals but hadn't stepped onto the podium with his back to a full concert hall. As for a national broadcast—it had been twenty years since an assistant had substituted for such an important concert. The musicians were anxious and the management apprehensive. Would this greenhorn save the day or besmirch the orchestra's reputation?

Ignoring the tension in Carnegie Hall, the young Bernstein bounded onto the podium and conducted a memorable performance. His talent was evident, his demeanor electrifying. This debut launched the nationally known career of the great Leonard Bernstein. In fifteen years he would be *the* New York maestro.

When Bernstein died a few years ago, his name was a

household word. His compositions, performances, broadcasts, books, and lectures made him America's most celebrated musician. Was his success just a matter of his having a "lucky break" one day when Walter was too sick to wave a baton?

No. Bernstein had more than "luck," so was it a matter of "luck" and *talent?*

No. It was more than that. From his youth, Bernstein had demonstrated a musical discipline like that of few others in his generation.

The morning after Bernstein's conducting debut, the *New York Times* featured the concert on the front page: "Young Aide Leads Philharmonic." And one of the reviewer's comments was how "remarkably free of his score" Bernstein was.

Though not expecting to conduct on that day, Bernstein was ready. What does "ready" mean? He'd spent years memorizing conducting scores—knowing what every instrument in the orchestra was playing and when.

As a student and an assistant, Bernstein had no promise that he would conduct these huge works in front of great crowds. Yet he put in the thousands of hours needed in case the situation ever presented itself. While fellow students were entertaining themselves, relaxing, or wasting time on diversions, the young Bernstein was diligently preparing for a lifetime of brilliance.

Some people "have faith" that they will meet with success, but they don't knuckle down with the discipline needed to prepare for the future.

Yet, preparedness is a key part of diligence, which the Bible repeatedly commends. Many people wait for a "great opportunity" to come their way, but opportunity has a way of making the unprepared look foolish.

Wise Solomon said, "He who works his land will have abundant food, but he who chases fantasies lacks judgment" (Prov. 12:11).

Stop for a second and consider your answer to this question: What am I working on today that will help me be more effective tomorrow?

Lord, help me be diligent today. But help me to trust You for tomorrow. Help me to prepare for the future without worrying about it. Forgive me when I fritter away the precious time I have to prepare myself for Your service. Help me to be ready for the opportunities You send my way—in Your good time.

If God is for us, who can be against us?
—Romans 8:31

Ruggiero Leoncavallo (1858–1919)

Believing the Best About Yourself

Italian composer Ruggiero Leoncavallo is known almost exclusively for one operatic masterpiece, *Pagliacci,* which made him a celebrity throughout his home country.

A good-natured fellow, Leoncavallo enjoyed playing pranks and "pulling people's legs," but at an opera house in Forli, Italy, he learned a hard lesson about the power of self-deprecating words.

Passing through Forli, he bought a ticket for a performance of his own *Pagliacci.* He assumed—or hoped—he wouldn't be recognized and "slipped in" without announcing himself. Who knows why he set out to see this production, because he watched with a seemingly bored disinterest. And this while the rest of the audience responded with wild enthusiasm.

He sat next to a young lady, who noticed his indifference. She leaned over and asked, "Don't you like it?"

Leoncavallo rejoined, "No, on the contrary, I find it great rubbish and unoriginal."

To her astonishment he went on and on, insisting that the composer copied this theme from Verdi and that theme from Wagner. He must have been laughing to himself as he tore his own opera to shreds.

The incredulous woman listened and then confirmed

what she'd heard. Leaving the performance, she asked, "And all that you have told me is your honest opinion of *Pagliacci?*"

"Yes, ma'am."

She walked away saying, "All right, one day you'll be sorry for it."

Imagine the composer's horror the next morning when he picked up the newspaper and saw the large headline: Leoncavallo On His Own Opera *Pagliacci!*

Many people, perhaps trying to display modesty, habitually "down themselves." Rather than receiving a well-intentioned compliment with a sincere "thank-you," some feel obliged to contradict the personal positive. Or some *always* give the credit away—to a parent, a spouse, a mentor, a colleague. The Scriptures speak clearly against prideful boasting, but there is a middle ground between bragging and self-deprecation.

Paul puts it all in perspective, affirming his competence but acknowledging that it comes from the Lord: "Not that we are competent to claim anything for ourselves, but our competence comes from God. He has made us competent as ministers of a new covenant" (2 Cor. 3:5–6).

If hearing personal praise is hard for you, try a new tack this week. If someone gives you a compliment for something you've done with excellence, try smiling. That in itself might be a big step. But then keep going and say a simple "thank-you." You might be surprised that you get a big smile in return.

Father, I want to give You a big smile and thank You for the gifts You have given me. Help me to receive with grace—not pride—the compliments others give me as I use those gifts for Your glory.

Serve wholeheartedly, as if you were serving the Lord, not men, because you know that the Lord will reward everyone for whatever good he does.
—Ephesians 6:7–8

Franz Schubert (1797–1828)

Excellence Versus Success

I recently visited the rather shabby house where Franz Schubert was born. Then I drove across Vienna, Austria, and saw the even shabbier house where he died. It was a profoundly moving experience. In his short thirty-one-year life, Schubert composed hundreds of the world's most beautiful songs, not to mention fantastic symphonies, sonatas, chamber music, and choral works—all while being virtually ignored and neglected by the world.

The great music that the poverty-stricken Schubert created seldom brought him any money. Even when he composed something that became popular in his time—such as his extraordinary song, the "Erl-King"—his lack of business experience prevented him from realizing appropriate profits. Having little financial sense, Schubert sold the "Erl-King" rights for a few hundred dollars.

Many of his greatest works were not even performed during his lifetime. For example, at one point Schubert completed two orchestra movements and sketched two more, presumably working out an entire symphony. For reasons unknown to history, he abandoned this project and sent away the manuscript. Nearly forty years after Schubert's death, one of his friends retrieved the score. Now known as Schubert's *Unfinished Symphony,* this work has become the most acclaimed musical fragment in all of music history.

Yet the lack of public accolades seemed to have no effect on the incredible output of this genius. Schubert once stated,

"When one piece is finished, I begin another." He even went to bed with his glasses on. The reason? He wanted to begin composing as soon as he awoke!

What enables a man to continue his toil without the external motivation of applause and wealth?

Schubert never strove for success; he strove for *excellence*. His motivation was simply to use his God-given talents to the best of his ability, whether anyone responded or not.

The relative obscurity of Schubert's short life gives us few details of his opinions and convictions. Yet the little we know testifies to a strong, personal faith in Christ, which sustained him through the years of unrewarded labor. His paramount audience was not the concertgoers or even his musical friends but the Lord Himself.

From time to time stop and ask yourself a hard question: "Would I be doing this if no one but God would ever know about it? Am I striving for excellence—to do my best for Christ—or for worldly success?" No matter how respectable our work may seem to our peers, the motives we bring to each task will be appraised by our supreme Rewarder. For "Man looks at the outward appearance, but the LORD looks at the heart" (1 Sam. 16:7).

Lord, thank You for the example of Franz Schubert. It reminds me that I am working for You. Forgive me when I become so concerned with the approval of others. Help me to concentrate on the excellence of my work, not on my "success." Help me to simply do my best and leave the results in Your hands.

Part Four

MUSICAL HUMILITY

The Key to Greatness

The greatest among you should be like the youngest,
and the one who rules like the one who serves.
Luke 22:26

I have endeavored to sink the language
to the level of a child's understanding.
—Isaac Watts

Johannes Brahms

JOHANNES BRAHMS (1833–1897)

Modesty Is the Best Policy

For by the grace given me I say to every one of you: Do not think of yourself more highly than you ought, but rather think of yourself with sober judgment, in accordance with the measure of faith God has given you.
—Romans 12:3

This German composer of great symphonies, songs, and chamber music was universally loved. And a principal, endearing quality was his unassuming modesty. Johannes Brahms would know world renown in his lifetime, becoming one of the most successful composers of the nineteenth century.

Yet even at the height of his fame, Brahms—who had been born in the slums of Hamburg—usually wore old, simple clothing; he enjoyed taking long country walks and eating in plain roadside cafés. He was a quiet benefactor to the poor around him, made friends easily, and was particularly fond of children. A bachelor, Brahms was unpretentious in his lifestyle. In fact, he grew the long bushy beard so prominent in his best portraits because he was tired of shaving and wearing ties!

In the midst of his unsought fame, which puzzled and amused him, Brahms was modest and unassuming about his creations. He once mailed—unregistered—the only existing manuscript copy of his Fourth Symphony to a conductor. In a fury, the conductor, Von Bulow, protested, "What would we have done had the packet gone astray?" Brahms simply stated, "In that case I would have to write the symphony anew."

But most revealing of Brahms's modesty are his comments comparing his music to that of other greats:

Concerning Mendelssohn, Brahms said, "I'd give all my compositions if I could have written such a piece as the *Hebrides Overture*."

After playing a Bach sonata, Brahms threw a copy of his own sonata on the floor: "After that, who could play such stuff as this?"

And at a dinner during which his host was about to toast "the health of the greatest composer," Brahms interrupted. Glass in hand he jumped to his feet and bellowed, "Quite right! Here's to Mozart's health!"

What a picture of unpretentious humility! Here is a man who had learned the profound truth of 1 Peter 5:5: "Clothe yourselves with humility toward one another, because, 'God opposes the proud but gives grace to the humble.'"

When I consider Brahms's life story, I think of a parable that Jesus told at a dinner when He "noticed how the guests picked the places of honor at the table":

> When someone invites you to a wedding feast, do not take the place of honor, for a person more distinguished than you may have been invited. If so, the host who invited both of you will come and say to you, "Give this man your seat." Then, humiliated, you will have to take the least important place. But when you are invited, take the lowest place, so that when your host comes, he will say to you, "Friend, move up to a better place." Then you will be honored in the presence of all your fellow guests. For everyone who exalts himself will be humbled, and he who humbles himself will be exalted (Luke 14:7–11).

What a wonderful story about the practical benefits of modesty. It may have its heavenly rewards, but in the here and now it can prevent humiliation. And I don't know anyone who doesn't want to avoid that hard lesson.

Father, help me to remember this parable that You taught to people who were "grabbing" for the most honored seats in the house. Give me a Brahms-type spirit of humility even in the midst of success. May I know when to keep silent and let my work or my character speak for itself.

Giuseppe Verdi (1813–1901)

Appealing Applause

The crucible for silver and the furnace for gold, but man is tested by the praise he receives.
—Proverbs 27:21

February 5, 1887—a red-letter date in opera history. The great Giuseppe Verdi hadn't composed an opera in fifteen years, but tonight the opera world was set to see his new work *Otello,* premiering at Milan's beautiful La Scala. *Otello* is perhaps Verdi's greatest opera—considered among the all-time best.

For this performance the audience came from all over Europe. And locally? Verdi was presented with a silver cup containing cards and autographs from *every* citizen of Milan.

After any successful premiere, a composer might expect to make a few bows, but Verdi was called for an unprecedented *twenty* ovations! Enthusiastic listeners tossed hats and handkerchiefs high in the air; many wept as they cheered the composer and his composition.

At long last the crowd started to disperse, and the composer left the opera house. Even then, Verdi was acclaimed. Fans had unhorsed Verdi's carriage and willingly wheeled him with their own manpower. Finally in his room alone, he still could not escape the applause. At five o'clock in the morning, the people were bellowing in the streets, "Viva Verdi!"

How did Verdi react to all this attention? Through the opera-house ovations, his calm face never moved a muscle. Reports claim that he appeared to be the only restrained person in the theater. Rather than bursting with pride, Verdi was unruffled, though somewhat embarrassed by the continuing bedlam.

This is not to say that Verdi was aloof or acted as if he felt superior to and condescending toward his fans. Haughtiness was not a part of this composer's makeup. Honors never turned his head. When the king offered to make him *Marchese di Busseto*, Verdi answered modestly, "Musician I was born, musician I remain." He was known to have many friends from all walks of life. He talked with kings in palaces and with organ-grinders on the streets.

Verdi had long since learned that life involves both triumph and rejection; neither mattered very much nor lasted for very long. Verdi had found that the important objective was simply to live one's life to the best of one's abilities, with or without victory. With this quiet resolution he moved on to write the finest comic opera of his career, *Falstaff*.

Often we think of failure and rejection as the most difficult "test" of our character, but sometimes the vanity of success can be the hardest assault on the humble faith God desires of us.

Who knows what applause you might receive this week or this year? Are you ready for it?

The wisdom of Solomon's Proverbs often strikes to the very heart of "real life." This is one of my favorites, especially when I consider the extent of Solomon's success and worldwide fame: "The crucible for silver and the furnace for gold, but man is tested by the praise he receives" (Prov. 27:21).

Lord, I admit that I find myself loving the sound of praise for my work. Help me to receive that applause with grace and humility. Help me to accept any praise and then quickly look ahead to the challenges of tomorrow—not boasting of my yesterdays.

Antonin Dvořák (1841–1904)

Content in Any Situation

I have learned the secret of being content in any and every situation.
—Philippians 4:12

Czech composer Antonin Dvořák learned to adapt his compositional talent to a variety of situations. He was determined to produce for nearly every genre, from concertos to chamber music, from solos to symphonies, from oratorio to opera. In fact, his entire life was to become a portrayal of adaptability.

As a young man, Dvořák was a typical provincial Bohemian boy. His father, a country innkeeper, struggled alongside his fellow countrymen, who were forced to lay aside higher aspirations just so they could put food on the table. The elder Dvořák, though a music lover who was proud of his son's obvious talent, could not justify Antonin's music training; his son should learn a trade that would guarantee an adequate income.

Despite his father's worries, Dvořák's musical career blossomed, making him an international traveler and a world-renowned celebrity.

Could this quiet, provincial man adapt to his new surroundings? How did his flight to fame affect him?

Dvořák accepted this new lifestyle with no apparent change to his personality, standards, or habits. He moved from rustic Bohemia to cosmopolitan New York City and yet remained a humble and honest man who profoundly loved God and his fellowman.

Even as an adult, Dvořák retained his youthful enthusiasm. Alongside music, of course, ocean liners and trains remained his lifelong passions. He cherished the company of all children. He loved animals, the outdoors, and games of any kind. The story is told of two of his friends talking about him. One of them lamented that Dvořák was obsessed with music and couldn't carry on a conversation about anything else. The other (closer) friend replied, "Did you try talking to him about pigs?"

Despite being uncomfortable in high social situations, Dvořák learned to "be himself" and make friends in any situation.

Easy for him, you might say. *But not for me. I'm no world traveler. I prefer staying in my own world where I know what's expected of me.*

But what if God should call you into a different circumstance or locale? Many would-be-great missionaries are defeated—not by hostile reception of the Gospel—but by their lack of ability in adapting to a foreign environment.

Today if you unexpectedly find yourself in an uncomfortably unfamiliar situation, think of Antonin Dvořák. Ask God to put you at ease; put your mind at ease knowing that God is with you. As the psalmist wrote, "If I settle on the far side of the sea, even there your hand will guide me, your right hand will hold me fast" (Ps. 139:9–10).

Father, thank You for being with me, always and everywhere. Forgive me when I fight against the circumstances You send my way. Help me to adapt myself to them, to grow through them, and to work within them for Your glory.

It is better to take refuge in the LORD than to trust in man. It is better to take refuge in the LORD than to trust in princes. . . . The LORD is my strength and my song; he has become my salvation.
—Psalm 118:8–9, 14

GEORGE FRÉDÉRIC HANDEL (1685–1759)

Beyond the Power Plays

On January 10, 1713, George Frédéric Handel premiered his only five-act opera, *Teseo*, at the Queen's Theatre in London. The performance was a smashing success, his second triumph since coming to England. Under what circumstances had he left Germany to come to the Isle? He was officially on leave from his employer, the elector of Hanover, who reluctantly allowed him to leave if he would return "in a reasonable time."

The opera's popularity introduced Handel to the aristocracy of London, including Queen Anne herself. She admired his music but also disdained Handel's boss in Hanover. She delighted in keeping his favorite musician in her country. Anne was so pleased by Handel's music—particularly after he wrote her a *Birthday Ode* that she gave him an annual pension of two hundred pounds. With the security of this royal patronage, Handel thought less often of his distant employer.

But as you may remember, Europe's history is a woven web of intrigue. And Queen Anne's patronage is not the end of the story. When Queen Anne died the next year, who should be crowned as her successor but Handel's disgruntled employer. The elector of Hanover became King George I of England!

Suddenly Handel was out of favor, not even called to the court. Was his career ruined because he'd banked on Queen Anne's support and not returned sooner to Germany?

A man of such talent and charm was able to arrange a reconciliation—some would say in classic Handelian style. The story is told that during a state aquatic pageant, Handel captivated his new monarch with a composition titled *Water Music*. A full orchestra performed on a barge floating down the Thames before King George, to his surprise and delight. Handel's *Water Music* soon moved from the barge to the concert hall and has captivated audiences ever since.

The story doesn't end even here. Handel outlived King George I, and the composer's popularity fluctuated wildly in coming years.

From this painful episode and others Handel learned about the fleeting nature of worldly success. He had a new understanding of his security being in God alone. After this he wrote much of his greatest music, particularly his masterpiece *Messiah*.

Whenever our work is well-received, it's all too easy to look to the person or group applauding our efforts, rather than to the Lord. But a wise person knows something about the shifting nature of favor and fame. Princes come and princes go—like fads and fortune.

When riding high, know that your confidence is not in your success. It is not dependent on some powerful person's opinion of you but in God—the King who reigns beyond worldly power plays.

Father, I praise You—the King who shall reign forever and ever. Thank You for any fulfillment I receive for works that bring glory to Your name. But I pray that my confidence will be based on the surety of Your kingdom—not on the shifting favor of men and women whose mortal "kingdoms" will fall.

Isaac Watts (1674–1748)

Welcome the Children and the Child in You

The disciples came to Jesus and asked, "Who is the greatest in the kingdom of heaven?" He called a little child and had him stand among them. And he said: "I tell you the truth, unless you change and become like little children, you will never enter the kingdom of heaven. Therefore, whoever humbles himself like this child is the greatest in the kingdom of heaven"
—Matthew 18:1–4

The adolescent fidgeted in his seat. The old pews were hard and the church service interminably long. But what bothered him the most was the pathetic singing, droning away at one note throughout a lengthy psalm. When he eventually complained, his father answered, "Give us something better, young man."

The young, bright Isaac Watts bit into the challenge as he had others: He started to study Latin at age four, Greek at nine, French at eleven, and Hebrew at thirteen. Now Isaac composed some simple hymns; he rewrote psalms to give them what he called a New Testament flavor. Years later, he would publish the popular *Psalms of David Imitated in the Language of the New Testament*.

Watts eventually became pastor of the Mark Lane Independent Chapel in London and was one of the finest preachers of his day, but unquestionably his greatest gift was hymnwriting. The singing of hymns was quite innovative at a time when only psalms had been sung in the "dissenting" (non-Anglican) churches of England.

Still considered the "father of English hymnody," Watts left a legacy of more than six hundred hymns, including *When I Survey the Wondrous Cross*, *Alas and Did My Savior Bleed*, *Joy to the World*, *Jesus Shall Reign*, and *Am I a Soldier of the Cross*?

Although a celebrated preacher, one of Watts's greatest joys was working with children, going to great lengths to simplify his language so that even the smallest child could appreciate God's ageless truths. Perhaps he remembered his own childhood and his adolescent complaint of the church's music. In time he wrote an entire book of hymns especially for youth: *Divine Songs Attempted in Easy Language for the Use of Children*. In that book he explained: "I have endeavored to sink the language to the level of a child's understanding." I can see that in the crisp, clear language of this song of praise:

I sing the mighty power of God,
That made the mountains rise,
That spread the flowing seas abroad,
And built the lofty skies.
I sing the wisdom that ordained
The sun to rule the day;
The moon shines full at his command,
And all the stars obey.

Jesus Himself was our model for welcoming children into His presence. What's more, when asked who is the greatest in His kingdom, He answered by saying that the greatest are those who humble themselves to become *like* little children. Children, who are in awe of the grandeur of God's creation. Children, who are vulnerable and counted among the weak. Children, who are pliable and trainable, looking to a "grown-up" for guidance and protection.

The greatest is like a child. What does that mean for you today?

Father, I stand before You as a small child reaching out and calling You "Abba" or "Daddy." I say this, yet I acknowledge that I don't always know what it means to be childlike—and yet mature in my Christian walk. Increase my understanding, my humility, and my welcoming spirit.

Johann Sebastian Bach (1685–1750)
Your Ultimate Audience

Humble yourselves before the Lord, and he will raise you up.
—James 4:10

On April 15, 1729, a little-known musician in Leipzig led the unassuming premiere of his latest work, the *Passion According to Saint Matthew*. The audience did not consist of royalty and high society. The performance was not booked in a renowned concert hall. The concert, featuring local singers and players, was given for the regular congregation, in the provincial church that employed Johann Sebastian Bach as its organist and composer in residence.

After Bach's death in 1750, this piece—along with virtually all of his music—would be forgotten. Even in his lifetime, his work hadn't been widely distributed—only ten of his original compositions were published. His work was performed before parishioners who could seldom tell a great work from a poor one and, as with the *Saint Matthew,* the musicians were often second-rate, not able to showcase his work.

Besides that, historically Bach was one of the last great masters of the Baroque period of composition. Musical tastes changed quickly after his death, and audiences wanted to forget the old and embrace the latest musical fashion.

Performances of his music ceased altogether. Precious manuscripts (priceless today) were lost, thrown away, or sold for a pittance. A whole bundle of cantatas is known to have once sold for the equivalent of forty dollars. And the great Brandenburg Concertos were valued at ten cents apiece by a

Brandenburg librarian. Some Bach manuscripts were even used as wrapping paper by local merchants and butchers! As you might well imagine, that means many works were lost forever—to the dismay of today's music lovers.

But Bach would not be forgotten forever. Greatness is always attracted to greatness, and Mozart found and enthusiastically studied several Bach manuscripts. Beethoven greatly admired some works by Bach. Knowing that the name "Bach" is the German word for *brook*, Beethoven once exclaimed, "Not 'Brook' but 'Ocean' should be his name!" A few years later, Franz Schubert noted in his diary, "Johann Sebastian Bach has done everything completely; he was a man through and through."

Almost exactly a century after its premiere, Bach's *Passion According to Saint Matthew* would be "discovered" by the young Felix Mendelssohn, prompting the great "Bach Revival" of the nineteenth century. Today, this work is universally considered a choral classic, performed all over the world, especially at Easter but also year-round.

How would Bach have reacted if he could have known of his music's eventual fame? No one knows for sure. But I am confident in saying that it would have baffled and amazed him. He lived a quiet life of service, was seldom in the public's eye, and received little recognition for his genius. Once, when someone praised his organ-playing skill, Bach simply said, "There is nothing very wonderful about it; you have only to hit the right notes at the right moment and the instrument does the rest."

What kept him going? Bach treated each work with the care of a master producing a renowned showpiece, knowing that he was preparing a work for a greater Master.

Often we do not get the recognition we deserve or desire.

When that happens, we can find inspiration—and courage—in the story of J. S. Bach who knew who his ultimate audience was.

The next time you're tempted to say, *Why am I doing this—going to all this effort—when no one ever notices?* think of Bach, the greatest musical genius, humbly writing for his local church and his Lord.

"Whatever you do, work at it with all your heart, as working for the Lord, not for men, since you know that you will receive an inheritance from the Lord as a reward. It is the Lord Christ you are serving" (Col. 3:23–24).

Lord, working without acclaim takes a vision and humility and that seems beyond my grasp. Who is my audience? Help me to see that it is You. Help me to make these words of Paul to the Colossian Christians my own, so that I can feel the joy of saying with confidence: "It is the Lord Christ I am serving!"

Humility and the fear of the LORD bring wealth and honor and life.
—Proverbs 22:4

FRANZ JOSEPH HAYDN (1732–1809)

Remembering Our Humble Roots

"When I sit at my old worm-eaten piano, I envy no king in his happiness." This statement of Franz Joseph Haydn, made when he was still young and unknown, illustrates the contentment and humility he retained long after he was acclaimed by the world. Being recognized as the world's greatest living composer was not Haydn's foundational "source of contentment."

This simple and modest man of faith was equally as humble when he was a poor youth playing for his supper in the streets of Vienna as he was years later as a renowned musician entertaining the royalty of Europe.

Living in a class-conscious society, Haydn chose to retain the lowliness of his early life long after the increase in his fame and fortune. Haydn often dressed as a peasant in his shirtsleeves, attending church with the common people. In the manner of a contented servant of God, Haydn answered one adoring fan: "Do not speak so to me. You see only a man whom God has granted talent and a good heart."

Late in life, he admitted, "I have associated with kings, emperors, and many great gentlemen and have heard many flattering things from them; but I do not wish to live on an intimate footing with such persons, and I prefer people of my own status."

Such a successful career might have invited a lesser man to an early retirement—to rest and enjoy the fruit of his labors. Yet Haydn continued to work through his last year. Three masterpieces, *The Seasons*, *The Seven Last Words of Christ*, and *The Creation*, were all composed late in life. Simplicity, generosity, and productivity exemplified his life to the very end.

I, too, in a "big city" world of music, often run into people who would like to conceal or forget their unimpressive beginnings. But those very beginnings are a part of who we are; to forget them is to forget how God used our early circumstances to shape us into what we are today. What's more, the humble memory of our past may keep us from being lured by the temptations of our present.

Isaiah's challenge is mine: "Listen to me, you who pursue righteousness and who seek the LORD: Look to the rock from which you were cut and to the quarry from which you were hewn" (Isa. 51:1). Who knows what beautiful sculpture can be cut from the stone in your family's quarry?

Father, I acknowledge that all my blessings have come from You. Help me never to be ashamed of my past circumstances but rather, to be thankful for all You have brought me through. As You have been with me in the past, Lord, I know that You will never forsake me in the future. Praise Your wonderful name!

Part Five

Musical Perseverance

If You Want to Succeed, Never Give Up

Let us throw off everything that hinders
and the sin that so easily entangles,
and let us run with perseverance the race marked out for us.
Hebrews 12:1

Ah! It seemed impossible for me to leave the world
until I had produced all that I felt called upon to produce.
—Ludwig van Beethoven

Giuseppe Verdi

Though my father and mother forsake me, the LORD will receive me.
—Psalm 27:10

GIUSEPPE VERDI (1813–1901)

Perseverance Before Success

March 11, 1851: The successful premiere of Giuseppe Verdi's eternally popular *Rigoletto*, at the Teatro La Fenice in Venice. In some ways the opera was a "long stretch." Based on Victor Hugo's play, "Le Roi s'amuse," the title role was a radical departure from the typical handsome leading tenor. Rigoletto was the hunchbacked jester to the Duke of Mantua. Initial and continued appreciation of the work stems largely from its many arias and its exquisite quartet.

The work established Verdi as a first-rate musician. It was his first great triumph—the first of many. But few people realize that this work was the composer's *sixteenth* opera! None of his previous efforts were received with much enthusiasm, and his finest compositions were created after *Rigoletto*. If Verdi had given up before 1851 (when he was thirty-eight years old), he would hardly have been remembered today. He might be a footnote in music history, the composer of fifteen mediocre operas.

But Verdi had become accustomed to rejection. As a young musician he had been humiliated when he was turned down at the Milan Conservatory; the entrance committee considered him "lacking in musical talent." Did he let this disgraceful rejection discourage him? Though disheartened,

he kept pursuing music and composition. And the music world is richer for his persistence.

In time, musical victories including *Rigoletto* made Verdi the most famous Italian composer of his day. He had such heroic acclaim that the monarch nominated him to be a senator in the Upper House—a position the modest composer quickly declined. Actually, he was a celebrity worldwide, evidenced by the fact that he sometimes received mail addressed simply, "Maestro Verdi, Italia."

Occasionally we hear of someone who is an overnight success—a first novel that hits the bestseller lists—a young, unknown recording artist who hits it big. But most of us walk a long, bumpy road to success or to perfecting our craft, and those bumps prepare us for the greater work ahead.

If you have not yet seen earthly reward for your work or art, don't give up. As you persevere, look to see what lessons you can learn from any constructive criticism you receive. Are there ways to improve your skills? Are there adjustments that would get you on a higher road? Is God simply asking you to wait for His good timing or to look to Him for your reward?

We can learn a great deal through rejection—as we persevere. I challenge you with the words of my father, who taught me that "the biggest mistake one ever makes is to quit."

God usually allows us to grow little by little until we are ready to blossom. But if we give up, we will never see the greater fruit that is to come.

Lord, You know how much it hurts to be rejected—even rejected without cause. Please help me as I persevere in my work, in my relationships, overcoming discouragements and disappointments. Help me to be renewed in spirit as I spend time with You—the One who will never leave or forsake me. Help me to accept the encouragement You offer me.

Ludwig Van Beethoven (1770–1827)

Perseverance in Work

As you know, we consider blessed those who have persevered.
—James 5:11

One's greatness is not defined merely by what one has achieved. Another question should be considered: What obstacles did this person overcome?

Ludwig van Beethoven possessed a tremendous resolve to persevere in the face of a musician's most terrible affliction: deafness.

Beethoven's music as well as his own written thoughts reveal the powerful convictions he maintained in the midst of trial and tragedy. He considered his talents a sacred trust from the Creator and strove to use them in the face of affliction compounded by humiliation and disgrace. He did not surrender to the difficulties and dejection created by his deafness. Over the years as his deafness worsened, his new compositions actually grew increasingly profound.

In Beethoven's day, deafness was a visible disability. If Beethoven wanted to hear anything clearly, he had to hold up a large, awkward ear-trumpet. This is a far cry from today's hearing aids, as unobtrusive as eyeglasses. And, in contrast to today's public, which is relatively accepting of physical handicaps, Beethoven's world was ignobly unsympathetic. Street urchins taunted and jeered as he shuffled through the streets of Vienna.

In a weak moment he wrote, "Alas! How could I possibly refer to the impairing of a sense which in me should have been more perfectly developed than in other people, a sense which at one time I possessed in the greatest perfection, even to a degree of perfection such as few in my profession possess or have ever possessed—oh, I cannot do it."

A friend related the sadness of a pitiful endeavor of Beethoven to play his beloved piano at a rehearsal of his *Archduke Trio*. "If it is a great misfortune for anyone to be deaf, how can a musician endure it without giving way to despair? Beethoven's continual melancholy was no longer a riddle to me."

Melancholy, yes, but Beethoven did not give up. The very tenacity that caused him to be seen as rude and discourteous enabled him to continue and even to expand his God-given compositional gifts. It is astounding to study the complexities and splendor of his late works and to realize that *he heard them only in his mind*, never by his natural ear.

Knowing his divine call, Beethoven wrote in his will, "Ah! It seemed impossible for me to leave the world until I had produced all that I felt called upon to produce."

But later in his diary, Beethoven reveals his heart's desire in a brief prayer: "In whatsoever manner it be, let me turn to Thee and become fruitful in good works."

Beethoven felt he was to fulfill a God-given purpose, as are we: "We are God's workmanship, created in Christ Jesus to do good works, which God prepared in advance for us to do" (Eph. 2:10).

If melancholy or discouragement is paralyzing you in some way, ask God to strengthen you. Then take one small spiritual step toward God and one small physical step toward some tangible goal. If God has given you a job to do, He will enable you to perform it no matter what hurdles block your path.

Today claim Paul's desire as your own: "I consider my life worth nothing to me, if only I may finish the race and complete the task the Lord Jesus has given me" (Acts 20:24).

Father, forgive me for becoming discouraged; sometimes the obstacles look like mountains. Give me strength to do Your work and a determined spirit that will never give up. Thank You for the inspiring testimony of Beethoven, and help me to persevere through every obstacle to Your glory.

Jacques Offenbach (1819–1880)

Perseverance in Hope

Wait for the LORD; be strong and take heart and wait for the LORD.
—Psalm 27:14

Raised in Germany, Jacques Offenbach became the master of the French operetta. Today his most performed work is the *Tales of Hoffman*, which, unfortunately, was premiered after his death. The story of an earlier composition, the operetta *Orpheus in the Underground*, can teach us an important and timeless lesson.

The public was initially indifferent to this operetta. A cool reception is hard on any artist's ego. In the performing arts it can mean a short run and a hard-wrought banishment to oblivion. *Orpheus* might have soon been withdrawn and forgotten by everyone if not for the pen of a powerful critic named Jules Janin. This outspoken critic was not indifferent at all—he utterly loathed the work! He attacked *Orpheus* with such enmity that Offenbach must have been sick with heartache when reading his newspaper. Of course there was nothing he could do to stop the denigrating assaults.

But Janin's censure took a curious twist: His fury simply piqued the curiosity of the public. They had to see what had prompted such outrageous criticism. Soon every performance was sold out. The operetta became the hottest topic of the year; everyone was singing Offenbach melodies. Most people in Paris disagreed with the critic's assessment and loved the music of *Orpheus*. At parties they would boast about how many times they had seen the production.

But think back to the beginning of the story: Without

the insulting reviews, most Parisians would never have heard the operetta. Finally, after 228 sold-out performances, the production stopped due to the musicians' exhaustion. The critic's painful attack had made Offenbach rich and famous.

Standing in the midst of a painful situation, it is nearly impossible to believe that "bad" can turn to "benefit." But we have a God whose ways are not our ways; we have a God who in all things works for our good.

David wrote Psalm 27—the lines that challenge us to "wait for the LORD." And David—far more than Jacques Offenbach—eventually knew the reality of God's ability to turn calamity into blessing.

If you are going through a trial, remind yourself of some previous time when a dream fell apart. Did your short-sightedness cause despair when you simply needed a long-distance view?

Until that time when you can see the clouds part, remember that "the LORD is close to the brokenhearted and saves those who are crushed in spirit" (Ps. 34:18). Lean into His love, and rest in the hope and peace that passes all understanding.

Father, You have a master plan that is more grand than anything I can imagine. With my human limitations I cannot see beyond today as You can. When today seems dark, help me to wait on You in faith and hope, knowing that my present and my future are in Your care.

He will have no fear of bad news; his heart is steadfast, trusting in the LORD.
—Psalm 112:7

BÉLA BARTÓK (1881–1945)
Perseverance in Composure

Béla Bartók was born in a small Hungarian town unpronounceably named *Nagyszentmiklos*. A child prodigy, he composed his first works at age nine. With his genius he composed some of the finest music of the twentieth century.

This man can be applauded for more than his masterful compositions. He exemplified an enviable even-tempered personality.

Perhaps the best illustration of Bartók's ability to remain calm in the midst of disaster occurred after the premiere of his work called *The Miraculous Mandarin,* at the time so innovative and outrageous that it was denounced and booed. The scandalized crowd threw stink bombs at the stage. The audience made so much noise that no one could really hear the music. The mayor of Cologne even demanded the resignation of the conductor, Eugen Szenkar.

The composer's reaction to such a fiasco? After the frenzied performance, Bartók calmly walked to the conductor's dressing room as if he were sauntering on a country vacation. Undisturbed by the rejection, he quietly said, "Eugen, on page 34, the second clarinet is marked *mezzo forte.* I couldn't hear it. Would you please mark it *forte?*"

This steady disposition would serve Bartók well in his last years, when he composed several of his greatest works while suffering from leukemia. Under physical duress—he had a fever for three entire years—he wrote his renowned *Concerto for Orchestra.* Bartók's productivity left no place for complaining. He worked until his dying day on his *Concerto for Piano No. 3.* He finished all but the last seventeen measures, which his students later finished.

Rudyard Kipling wrote an inspiring poem titled "If," listing line after line of qualities that distinguish a man from a boy. Here's two of my favorite lines:

> If you can meet with Triumph and Disaster
> And treat those two impostors just the same . . .

A mature person can pull up an internal strength to keep his or her head in the midst of crisis. It's a grace that can be ours through faith as we look beyond the disaster to One who wants to steady us on our journeys.

The Christian's imperturbable spirit can be found in the knowledge of God's character and promises. Consider: "When you pass through the waters, I will be with you" (Isa. 43:2). In a passage about the "unchanging nature" of God and His purpose, the writer of Hebrews uses a powerful image, saying that we have "an anchor for the soul, firm and secure" (Heb. 6:19). And James 1:17 says He "does not change like shifting shadows."

As you face the unknown challenges of the day, think about the phrase that titles this piece: "Perseverance in Composure." What does it mean for you?

Lord, I want to have a steadfast heart and be someone who does not shift as sand in the wind or a boat on stormy waves. But left to myself, I am too weak to have such strength of character. I ask You to strengthen my faith, my steadfastness, my confidence in Your steady unshifting presence.

HORATIO SPAFFORD (1828–1888)

Perseverance in Faith

My soul finds rest in God alone; my salvation comes from him. He alone is my rock and my salvation; he is my fortress, I will never be shaken.
—Psalm 62:1–2

Misfortune wasn't new to Horatio Spafford. In 1871 the great Chicago fire destroyed his massive real estate holdings on the shore of Lake Michigan. The financial fallout was horrendous, but he consoled himself that at least his family was safe.

Just two years later, the Spafford family—Horatio, his wife, and their four young daughters—looked forward to a needed break, accompanying friends to Europe, crossing the Atlantic on the *Ville du Havre*.

At the last minute, however, business concerns unexpectedly held Mr. Spafford in Chicago. He sent the family ahead of him, assuring them he would follow as soon as he could and meet them in France.

But that was not to be. In the mid-Atlantic the *Ville du Havre* collided with an English ship and sank in only twelve minutes. All four of the Spafford girls drowned; only Mrs. Spafford was named among the survivors.

I have four children. The thought of receiving such a telegram as was given to Horatio Spafford—I can't get near it. Horatio immediately headed for New York and boarded a slow boat to his wife's side. The ship's captain knew of the father's grief and one day called Horatio on deck to tell him, "To the best of my calculations, Mr. Spafford, this is where your daughters were drowned."

What were Horatio's thoughts as he gazed into the watery grave? Later that very day he wrote down his emotions—neither a lament nor a complaint, neither anger nor remorse.

When peace like a river attendeth my way,
When sorrows like sea billows roll;
Whatever my lot, thou hast taught me to say,
It is well, it is well with my soul.

Here was a man who persevered in faith despite misfortune that is hardly imaginable to me—and maybe to you. Yet his faith rested firmly in the God of his salvation.

The writer of Hebrews challenges us to *perseverance* in the context of faith:

> Let us run with perseverance the race marked out for us. Let us fix our eyes on Jesus, the author and perfecter of our faith, who for the joy set before him endured the cross, scorning its shame, and sat down at the right hand of the throne of God. Consider him who endured such opposition from sinful men, so that you will not grow weary and lose heart (Heb. 12:1–3).

To this day the witness of Spafford's song reminds believers to fix their eyes on the author and perfecter of their faith, the God of their salvation.

Father, thank You for these words, which calm my spirit even as I sing them. Through Your Son's death and resurrection, You have assured my salvation. Help me to rest in that salvation even as I persevere in faith and continually claim: "It is well with my soul."

Dmitri Shostakovich (1906–1975)

Perseverance Under Persecution

Be strong and courageous. Do not be afraid or terrified because of them, for the LORD your God goes with you; he will never leave you nor forsake you.
—Deuteronomy 31:6

Twentieth-century Russia has a paradoxical history. On one hand, the Russian people have a deep love of the arts and their great artistic heritage. On the other hand, governmental authority and misrule cruelly stifled artistic creativity in favor of "the party line."

Into such turmoil was born one of Russia's most talented and productive composers, Dmitri Shostakovich. His early symphonies and many piano works earned him the title "composer-laureate of the Soviet State."

But Shostakovich's official praises did not long endure. His innovative music soon raised eyebrows, including the bushy eyebrows of Stalin himself. On January 28, 1936, Shostakovich picked up the Soviet newspaper, *Pravda*, to read an official review of his music. The title: "Muddle Instead of Music."

The party branded Shostakovich as the "enemy of the people" (a phrase originating with Stalin), and the entire Russian government aimed propaganda guns at him. Meetings were organized to poison the public's opinion of him. People threw stones at his windows. When he arranged for a concert, the paper announced, "Today there will be a concert by the enemy of the people Shostakovich." Foes and friends expected a bad end to come for him, and quickly.

Nevertheless, Shostakovich was not ever frightened into

paralysis. Instead, he patiently kept writing his remarkable music, all the while trying to work with the government. Rather than provoking more vehemence, he tried a conciliatory tone. He humbly called his *Fifth Symphony* "a Soviet artist's practical, creative reply to just criticism."

In time such longsuffering was rewarded. He was never completely censured, and as he continued writing new, quality works, his international fame spread. The party finally acquiesced to Shostakovich's world-class stature and essentially left him alone.

At home the Russian people admitted their love for his work, and his premieres became instant sell-outs. He even became the first composer whose work was performed extraterrestrially. To mission control on April 12, 1961, cosmonaut Yuri Gagarin sang Shostakovich's song, "My Homeland Hears, My Homeland Knows Where in the Skies Her Son Soars On."

With such a hostile government against him, Shostakovich had every reason to shut down his "production," but persecution seemed to fuel his outstanding productivity. He didn't stop when his *Fourth Symphony* was officially condemned; in fact, he wrote *fifteen* symphonies in all (more than any major composer since Mozart!).

How do you respond when external forces threaten your work or your ministry? What if someone suddenly decided you were the "enemy of the people"? Would you dig a hole and "cease and desist"?

When the disciples in Acts 4 learned that their government was against them, their prayer was for the boldness and courage to persevere. It can be our prayer as well.

Father, nothing is too difficult for You. You have protected and emboldened Your saints for centuries. Help me as I face criticism and harsh words. Enable me to persevere with a boldness that is from You.

Whatever your hand finds to do, do it with all your might.
—Ecclesiastes 9:10

Wolfgang Amadeus Mozart (1756–1791)

Perseverance Under Pressure

In his short life of thirty-five years, Wolfgang Amadeus Mozart created more music than most composers who lived to be ninety. He produced a huge quantity of compositions: Symphonies, chamber music, Masses, concerti, songs, and operas all flowed from his pen with amazingly little effort. "Composition is less tiring than doing nothing," he said, explaining his astonishing musical output.

Mozart was more than a genius; he was an industrious, hard worker. He often worked out a piece of music in his mind as he went about a day's activities. Then when he sat down to a piece of music paper, he quickly "copied out" the notes that were in his head.

This was a man who frequently worked long night hours. The story behind the overture to his opera *Don Giovanni* is not untypical. Although performed as an introduction, the overture is often written after the rest of the opera. The overture weaves together all the main themes of the opera in an exciting instrumental setting.

Because of various time pressures, Mozart didn't begin writing the overture to *Don Giovanni* until the night *before* its first performance! The deadline was firm. He had to give the finished score to the copyist by 7:00 A.M. so that the individual instrumental parts could be copied out during the day for the orchestra members.

As he often did, Mozart prevailed upon his wife, Constance,

for help. Stirring up his favorite punch, she amused him with stories and jokes to keep him awake while he composed. But after so many tales of Aladdin's lamp and Cinderella, the composer started to doze off. Finally, Constance convinced him to take a one-hour nap.

Unfortunately, he slept so soundly that his wife didn't have the heart to wake him until five o'clock. Two hours to go!

Many other composers would have either given up or produced rubbish. Not Mozart. At seven o'clock the copyist received the score—a score of such musical genius that it is still a great favorite.

The ink on the orchestra parts was barely dry at the evening premiere and, of course, the overture was completely unrehearsed, but the ever-enthusiastic Mozart mounted the podium and conducted the orchestra with gusto. The audience was enraptured by the work, and the composer was delighted with the orchestra's sight-reading abilities. He applauded them with a "Bravo, bravo, gentlemen! That was excellent!"

In any field we are sometimes asked to perform under tremendous pressure. We get out of school and think the days of "cramming" for exams are over, but that outside push of deadlines is likely to trail us for the rest of our lives. Have you ever had a panicked dream: *Tomorrow is graduation day and I still have three papers to write! How am I going to finish my work in such short time?*

We can take a lesson from Mozart, who pushed himself and persevered under pressure to finish a work in progress. Surely an element of his genius was his willingness to keep working when others would have given up—and his ability to produce and not panic when under pressure.

At the end of his letter to the Colossians, Paul exhorts a

friend, "Tell Archippus: 'See to it that you *complete the work* you have received in the Lord'" (Col. 4:17).

Of course, we are not superhuman. We are not even Mozarts, for he is among the all-time greats in his productivity. Even Mozart didn't work through every night; neither can you or I. And the Scriptures clearly establish the need for our rest, and for setting priorities.

But when we are faced with deadlines, we can be challenged by Mozart, who did not panic when the pressure was on but persevered.

As you face a deadline today—or next week—know that panic is not your solution. Plug away. Seek solutions. Know that God's grace is "tighter"—closer to you—than your deadline.

Father, it is hard for me to work productively to finish a project under pressure. When I want to give up, please be there and give me grace to keep going. Help me to know the satisfaction that comes with having completed a job well-done.

Part Six

Musical Generosity

Give It Away and You Will Have It All

A generous man will prosper;
he who refreshes others will himself be refreshed.
Proverbs 11:25

Messiah *has fed the hungry, clothed the naked, fostered the orphan . . . more than any other single musical production in this or any country.*

—A. E. Bray, concerning the substantial funds that George Frédéric Handel donated from benefit concerts of his oratorio *Messiah*

George Frédéric Handel

GEORGE FRÉDÉRIC HANDEL (1685–1759)

Beyond Greed, Meeting Need

Honor the LORD with your wealth, with the firstfruits of all your crops; then your barns will be filled to overflowing, and your vats will brim over with new wine.
—Proverbs 3:9–10

By the end of his life, George Frédéric Handel was a rich man with an adoring public and worldwide acclaim. But previously, for decades, he had struggled with failure, at times being so financially strapped that he was threatened with debtors' prison.

As an older, successful man, Handel did not forget his impoverished past. Rather, he chose to use his fortune as a means to help others less fortunate. The story behind his masterpiece *Messiah* reflects Handel's generosity.

The oratorio was commissioned by a Dublin charity wanting to premiere a piece for a benefit concert. That first performance, on April 13, 1742, raised four hundred pounds, enough to free 142 men from debtors' prison. This charitable event was just the first for what has become a true classic.

Handel himself conducted the *Messiah* more than thirty times, many of these concerts being benefits for a favorite charity, the Foundling Hospital. In his will, Handel stipulated that this work was to continue to be used for the hospital's benefit.

The success of such charity performances prompted one biographer to say, "*Messiah* has fed the hungry, clothed the naked, fostered the orphan . . . more than any other single musical production in this or any country." Another wrote, "Perhaps the works of no other composer have so largely contributed to the relief of human suffering."

I like to think that God wanted to give Handel a sign of

His special blessing on this inspired work—and a sign of His approval for Handel's fiscal generosity and benevolence. If you've been to a live performance of *Messiah,* you may have wondered why the audience stood up on the first notes of the brilliant "Hallelujah Chorus." The practice goes back to 1743, a year after the oratorio's Dublin premiere. In London, the king of England attended a performance conducted by Handel. The king was so moved by the triumphant "hallelujah" that he rose to his feet. The entire audience followed his lead, initiating a tradition that still stands. Might God in His otherworldly ways have designed this unprecedented practice as His sign of blessing on the composer?

If your talent in any area brought you wealth if not fame, how would you respond? What would you do with that wealth? Would you simply increase your standard of living, buy a bigger house, upgrade your car and other "toys"? Or would you use it to meet the needs of others who have not known your good fortune?

Perhaps the answer to this hypothetical question is found in another question: What am I doing *right now* with the wealth God has given me? How am I using what I have at my disposal to help others? Jesus said, "Where your treasure is, there your heart will be also" (Matt. 6:21). It's easy to say rather flippantly that we want our hearts to belong wholly to the Lord. But when we make the foundational connection between heart and treasure, the commitment becomes more serious, harder to make.

Take a moment to examine your heart. Ask God for His grace to open your heart and your hands. Remember that all we have is from Him. "Every good and perfect gift is from above" (James 1:17). "Freely you have received; freely give" (Matt. 10:8).

Lord, I'm often like a toddler saying, "Mine, mine," or, "More, more." Forgive me for my greed and remind me often that every good gift I have is from You. Lord, let me be openhanded, willing to share my treasure in a way that will bring You glory and bless others.

Peter Illych Tchaikovsky (1840–1893)

If Not for Your Support

See that you also excel in this grace of giving.
—2 Corinthians 8:7

Tchaikovsky is one of the greatest composers that Russia has ever produced. His many popular works include the *Nutcracker Suite*, the *1812 Overture*, the *Romeo and Juliet Overture*, and the *Sleeping Beauty* and *Swan Lake* ballets. His six magnificent symphonies are in the repertoire of every major orchestra.

A hundred years after Tchaikovsky's death, his name is universally recognized among the greats. But do you recognize the name *Nadezhda Filaretovna von Meck*? Probably not.

Yet, without her, Tchaikovsky's masterpieces might never have been written. Who was she? Madame von Meck was a rather untalented but wealthy woman who never met Tchaikovsky in person. A fervid music lover, she became Tchaikovsky's greatest patron and musical advocate; for thirteen years she gave him a bountiful stipend, enabling him to devote himself entirely to honing his compositional talent.

Where would Tchaikovsky's music be without Madame von Meck's unselfish support? Who knows? It might have been buried with him, never having been performed or written on paper for posterity.

In every generation some people are blessed with talent and a vision for what they could accomplish if resources were available. Most of us know someone in such a position, perhaps starting a church, beginning a new career or entrepreneurial business, embarking on a missionary venture—or an

artistic venture. But without the love, endorsement, or backing of others, even the most indomitable pathfinders may succumb to discouragement and relinquish their tasks.

Words of encouragement and praise can be very meaningful, but sometimes words are not enough as we "consider how we may spur one another on toward love and good deeds" (Heb. 10:24).

You may not be as rich as Madame von Meck, but consider what you *can* do to encourage someone you know who has talent and vision. Ask God to give you a glimpse of someone's potential and to show you how you can help.

Perhaps your praise and generosity will "spur" another "Tchaikovsky."

Father, give me a glimpse of the potential You see in someone's talent and vision. Show me whom I should encourage, pray for, and support. And show me how I should help, in the way that would honor You and best use the resources You have given me.

Johann Sebastian Bach (1685–1750)

It Could Be a Bach

A generous man will himself be blessed, for he shares his food with the poor.
—Proverbs 22:9

In the country of Saxony in the seventeenth and eighteenth centuries, the name *Bach* was practically synonymous with the word *music*. More than fifty noteworthy musicians bore that name. But the greatest of them all—and father or grandfather of many—was Johann Sebastian.

Even as a boy he eagerly sought out expression and training of his emerging musical talent. On several occasions he set out to walk from Luneburg to Hamburg to hear the renowned organist Reincken and try to learn his secrets. On one of those treks when he was an older teen, Bach's enthusiasm overspent his meager pocketbook. He left Hamburg to return home with only two shillings in his pocket.

When still far from home, he was so hungry that he could hardly put one foot in front of the other. To rest, he sat down in front of a roadside inn, where the kitchen aromas almost drove him mad.

I can only imagine that the devout Bach prayed that God would come to his aid, but even so, he was surprised by the ways and means of His provision: It seems that some kind soul in the kitchen had noticed the forlorn youth. Someone opened a window and threw toward the boy two herrings' heads, a real delicacy in those regions! As Bach ravenously gobbled them up, he came upon his second blessing. In each

of the fish he found a Danish ducat coin—more than enough to get him home comfortably.

Bach was overcome with joy and thankfulness. One can almost see him dancing down the road in delight, his supper in one hand and his coins in the other. His anonymous benefactor must have smiled warmly as he or she peeked out the window, sending the boy rejoicing on his way.

The writer of Hebrews encourages us to be generous with strangers: "Do not forget to entertain strangers, for by so doing some people have entertained angels without knowing it" (Heb. 13:2). And James asks a challenging question: "Suppose a brother or sister is without clothes and daily food. If one of you says to him, 'Go, I wish you well; keep warm and well fed,' but does nothing about his physical needs, what good is it?" (James 2:15–16).

These days we are so often warned against charlatans and violence that we can become cold to the needs of strangers, especially those who are poor. Then sometimes we're just in too much of a hurry to pay attention to anyone who isn't "important."

I'm not saying that every stranger's request is my—or your—responsibility to meet, but we need to be open to the leading of the Holy Spirit. Today someone I meet might be one of the "least of these" with whom Christ identified. It might be an "angel unawares," to use a King James phrase. It might be a musical virtuoso in the midst of hard times, in need of a meal.

Father, I ask that You give me discernment—to be harmless as a dove and wise as a serpent in my response to strangers. Help me to recognize the prompting of the Holy Spirit and be ready to respond with a spontaneous gift to someone who might be a stranger to me but well-known to You.

HECTOR BERLIOZ (1803–1869)

Thank You with No Restraint

Dear children, let us not love with words or tongue but with actions and in truth.
—1 John 3:18

The composer Hector Berlioz stood in awe of the virtuosity of Niccolò Paganini (1782–1840), the greatest violinist of his day. In 1834 Berlioz composed a work for orchestra and viola soloist—Paganini. Its title, *Harold in Italy,* refers to "Childe Harold," a romantic poem by Lord Byron.

As things turned out, *Harold* was performed by several musicians before Paganini actually heard the piece. When he did, he immediately insisted on meeting the composer.

He did so backstage after a performance of *Harold* conducted by Berlioz himself. Neither man was in top shape that day. Berlioz was trembling with exhaustion from the intense performance, and Paganini could barely speak due to a severe throat infection.

Nevertheless, an animated Paganini whispered to his son, Achille, who turned to Berlioz and announced, "My father desires me to assure you, sir, that he has never in his life been so powerfully impressed by a concert; that your music has quite moved him, and that if he did not restrain himself he should go down on his knees to thank you for it."

Paganini may have restrained himself and stayed on his feet, but he acted on his enthusiasm by kissing Berlioz's hand before many onlookers.

Certainly this dramatic honor was a profound encouragement to Berlioz, but that incident is not the end of the story.

At this time in his life, the public was slow to reward Berlioz for his innovative compositions, and his family had many material needs. The distinguished violinist's encouragement went beyond words into action.

The next day, Paganini's son delivered an envelope to the composer's home. Inside it, Berlioz and his wife found twenty thousand francs. Mrs. Berlioz called for their son to join in the celebration: "Come here! Come here and thank God for what He has done for your father." The mother and son fell on their knees in gratitude to God.

When I stop to think of the many ways in which colleagues, friends, even strangers have been generous to me, I want to lose restraint and drop to my knees—to thank them and to thank God for His goodness. Sometimes the generosity is not monetary but a gift that shows me honor or respect. Sometimes it is an act of kindness that turns around a "bad day." How about you? Is there someone whose generosity merits a big thanks? Go ahead, say it—today.

Father, I thank You for Your generosity to me—a generosity that often is delivered through Your people. Today, help me to free up an extra moment in my schedule so I can make one phone call of appreciation to someone who's been generous to me. I pray that You will use that "thank-you" to increase someone else's gratitude—to You and in turn to others.

FANNY CROSBY (1820–1915)

God's Anonymous Partner

A generous man will prosper; he who refreshes others will himself be refreshed.
—Proverbs 11:25

Blind from the age of six weeks, Fanny Crosby wrote the lyrics for more than eight thousand gospel songs in her long life. You're probably familiar with some of her classics: "Blessed Assurance," "To God Be the Glory," "Draw Me Nearer," "Rescue the Perishing," "Safe in the Arms of Jesus," and "Near the Cross." One of my favorites is "All the Way My Savior Leads Me."

Crosby's way with words was bolstered by a phenomenal familiarity with the poetic King James Bible. By time she was twelve, she had memorized the five books of the Pentateuch, Ruth, Song of Solomon, all of Proverbs, and many psalms.

Crosby—Mrs. Alexander Van Alstyne—may have hidden God's Word in her heart, but she did not hold tightly to her worldly goods. She made the conscious choice to live among the poor and to be one with them, making her home in a small apartment in Lower Manhattan, not far from the famed Bowery Mission. She generously entertained neighbors, welcoming them by singing her songs. Like the widow of the Gospels, she gave away what she had with little thought for her own needs.

But her needs dramatically surfaced one day late in 1874; Crosby had to face the sober truth that she didn't have enough cash to pay the due rent. She was ten dollars short.

Crosby was not a solitary woman. She could have called on any number of wealthy friends gained through her musi-

cal fame. But no. She chose to take her need directly to the Lord. Fervently she prayed that God would meet this need—in His way and for His glory. It wasn't long before Crosby heard a knock on the door. When she opened it, someone pressed a folded ten-dollar bill into her hand and left without a word.

Who was the mystery donor? Blind Crosby had no idea but she did know who was responsible for the delivery. That afternoon she sat down and wrote these words:

All the way my Savior leads me;
What have I to ask beside?
Can I doubt His tender mercy,
Who through life has been my guide?

Heavenly peace, divine comfort,
Here by faith in Him to dwell!
For I know whate'er befall me
Jesus doeth all things well.

When I read or hear this song, I am moved to thank God for His care and guidance. I also think of the anonymous giver whose ten-dollar gift God used to inspire such poetry and the faith behind it.

Maybe God wants you to be part of a miracle today—by anonymously giving someone a gift of time or money or simple kindness. Consider the Lord's words: "When you give to the needy, do not let your left hand know what your right hand is doing, so that your giving may be in secret. Then your Father, who sees what is done in secret, will reward you" (Matt. 6:3–4).

What might that reward be? You never know what hymn of praise you may secretly inspire—maybe a classic that the church will sing through the twenty-first century!

Father, You have been generous to me. Today help me to see an opportunity to be generous in a way that gives You the glory and keeps me in the background, out of sight. Let me be the anonymous partner in Your scheme of grace.

WOLFGANG AMADEUS MOZART (1756–1791)

A Friend Indeed

Be imitators of God, therefore, as dearly loved children and live a life of love, just as Christ loved us and gave himself up for us as a fragrant offering and sacrifice to God.
—Ephesians 5:1–2

Many great composers, including Beethoven, Haydn, and Debussy, composed masterpieces slowly and laboriously, but Wolfgang Amadeus Mozart had a particular gift of creating with astonishing speed. One of the quickest composers in history, he often wrote incomparable works in a matter of hours and was known to have used this ability in the service of others.

Mozart was a close friend of the composer Michael Haydn (brother of the eminent composer Franz Joseph Haydn). Not a rich man, Michael Haydn once received a desirable commission to write some duets for violin and tenor—but on a very short deadline. Under normal circumstances the resourceful Haydn could have met this deadline, but at the critical moment he became incapacitated by illness and feebly lay on his bed—as sick with worry as with his ailment.

When Mozart heard that his friend would lose money due to this misfortune, he went to Haydn's bedside and undertook the task himself. Ignoring the sick friend's protests, Mozart worked as if the commission were his own. It goes without saying that the duets were completed in ample time—and masterfully so.

Such a charitable action was characteristic of Mozart. Though he could have used the money himself, he did the job without accepting any payment. His magnanimity did not

end there. He insisted that these duets be presented under Haydn's name, giving him not only the money but the credit for their excellent composition. It was years before the truth was made public, and these lovely duets are today in the *Mozart* catalogs, listed as K.423 and K.424.

Mozart modeled a generosity hard to find in our fast-paced generation. We often make a halfhearted offer, "Anything I can do, just let me know," and walk away perhaps hoping that we'll never be called.

But despite protests and a schedule of his own to keep, Mozart stepped in and helped a friend through a dark day.

That's the kind of generosity the Christian community can use more of—*being* there, bearing one another's burdens, modeling the love of Christ.

Lord, give me a servant's heart, and give me eyes to discern when I should step in, serving my friends, meeting their needs.

Ludwig van Beethoven (1770–1827)

A Suitable Gift

Each man has his own gift from God.
—1 Corinthians 7:7

In 1818, Londoner Thomas Broadwood wanted to show his admiration for the composer Ludwig van Beethoven. What would the great master like?

What else? A new grand piano! And not just *any* piano. Before sending this wonderful present, Broadwood had several prominent pianists test it. As if it were a stamp of approval, Clementi, Cramer, Ries, and other distinguished men wrote their names inside the instrument.

Broadwood's generosity did not end here. He arranged with the Court of Exchequer to waive the piano's import duty. Thomas Broadwood knew how to bless someone with the perfect gift.

Beethoven was overwhelmed! History has preserved the composer's exhilarated letter of thanks to his London benefactor. This thank-you letter—written in French—overflows with enthusiastic gratitude. The note begins "Mon Très Cher Ami Broadwood!" That might not need interpretation, but here it is: "My very dear friend Broadwood!"

Music history gives us no other glimpses of Thomas Broadwood, but from this episode it is clear that he was a generous man who gave "the right gift"—one that suited the needs and interests of the receiver.

There's a certain delight that comes from receiving a gift that's obviously been bought or made with our unique personalities and interests in mind. And there's a similar joy in

being the giver—who loves someone enough to give that "perfect" gift that says "I know you and love you."

Who knows us better than the One who knit us together in the womb—our Creator? He generously gives His children unique gifts and graces, each to be used for His glory. Some of these gifts are talents or material gifts. Some are spiritual: "There are different kinds of gifts, but the same Spirit. . . . All these are the work of one and the same Spirit, and he gives them to each one, just as he determines" (1 Cor. 12:4, 11).

How has God uniquely gifted you to allow you to become all you were meant to be? How can you thank Him—as your "très cher ami"?

Father, I thank You for the specific gift of ________, which brings me great delight. It also gives me a responsibility to use the gift to Your glory. Help me as I make every attempt to use this gift wisely. Allow me to get a glimpse of the joy You have in giving Your children the perfect gift that suits their needs and temperaments.

Part Seven

MUSICAL COURAGE

The One Thing That Will Banish Your Fears

Have I not commanded you?
Be strong and courageous.
Do not be terrified; do not be discouraged,
for the LORD your God will be with you wherever you go.
Joshua 1:9

There is no greater stimulus
for artistic work than suffering.
—Zoltan Kodály

Nicholay Rimsky-Korsakov

NICHOLAY RIMSKY-KORSAKOV (1844–1908)

Courage to Accept a New Challenge

The LORD turned to him and said, "Go in the strength you have . . . Am I not sending you?"
—Judges 6:14

As a boy growing up in the Russian town of Tilhvin, Nicholay Rimsky-Korsakov was attracted to music, but that largely untrained interest did not seem a career possibility when he went to sea to serve in the czar's navy.

Yet the fascination didn't die. During long stretches aboard ship, he let his mind trifle with music; while off-duty he would outline musical scores.

Then one on-shore day in 1865 changed the course of his life. Docked in St. Petersburg, he met a number of musician friends who urged him to complete a symphony he had sketched in his spare time. Their challenge set him to work. With some trepidation, he soon handed his friends a finished piece. They delivered it to an orchestra, which played the premiere—a smashing success!

With this encouragement, Rimsky-Korsakov wrote new compositions. Despite his friends' praise, he was still unsure about his work. After all, he was just a sailor who tinkered with music, having had little formal musical training.

Imagine his stupefaction when, in 1871, his friends asked him to accept a new job—as professor of composition at the St. Petersburg Conservatory! He remembers, "At the time, I could not even harmonize a chorale properly." Nevertheless,

professionals were asking him to lead one of Russia's foremost musical establishments.

Should he take the plunge? It seemed almost as dangerous as jumping overboard at sea. The challenge was surely beyond his capabilities—and yet friends he trusted kept telling him he could do it.

Finally, with fear and trembling, he accepted the post, studying strenuously to make up for lost time. Long after he'd left students and classrooms and administrative responsibilities, he would toil through the night to teach himself.

The professor's fears were needless; in time he convinced his greatest critic (himself) that he was quite capable for the task. His own studying gave him an extra empathy for his young students, and his long tenure proved a successful career change. He became one of the greatest teachers in the Conservatory's history. Rimsky-Korsakov and his colorful technique influenced students such as Glazunov and Stravinsky—renowned Russian composers of the next generation.

As for his own compositions, you might know some of his best-known orchestra scores, *Scheherazade* (based on the *Arabian Nights* stories), the *Capriccio Espagnol*, and the *Russian Easter Overture* (based on themes prominent in the Russian Orthodox Church).

If you are suddenly confronted with an assignment that makes you feel "not good enough," take it to the Lord. If it is not His will, ask Him to make that clear to you. But if you believe that God is in this opportunity, be brave. Set out in faith that the Lord will enable you to go through the doors He opens. As Moses reassured the Israelites just before the parting of the Red Sea: "Stand firm and you will see the deliverance the LORD will bring you today" (Exod. 14:13).

Father, when opportunity knocks, sometimes I feel utterly inadequate to accept the challenge. Especially when I feel fear and am unsure of myself, help me to know whether I should open the door. Give me the confidence that comes from You.

For God hath not given us the spirit of fear; but of power, and of love, and of a sound mind.
—2 Timothy 1:7 KJV

ARNOLD SCHOENBERG (1874–1951)

Courage to Say No—When No Makes No Sense

Arnold Schoenberg, an innovative composer years ahead of his time, was not a wealthy man. Born in Vienna, Austria, he lived in Berlin when Hitler was first coming to power. Like thousands of others, he was aware of the ominous political speeches but hoped against hope that things would calm down. As he waited for that day, he eked out a living and continued to write his imaginative music.

With his wife as librettist, Schoenberg composed a one-act comic opera called *Von Heute auf Morgen* ("From Day to Day"). Unfortunately, its premiere was not well-performed; the disapproving composer addressed the orchestra, "Gentlemen, the difference between what you have played tonight and what I wrote in my score would make a new opera!"

But this very composition soon presented the Schoenbergs with the opportunity—or temptation—of a lifetime. In those uncertain political times, when they were hardly able to pay their monthly bills, the Schoenbergs were unexpectedly offered the huge sum of one hundred thousand reichsmarks for the rights to publish their opera. But the deal had a strange stipulation. The publisher insisted, "I'm leaving tomorrow; you'll have to decide within ten minutes."

So in a private office, the husband and wife team conferred about the curious offer. Arnold wasn't comfortable with the time pressure, but one hundred thousand reichsmarks was far more than he had ever been offered for his music. His wife was cautious: "I don't like the way this man is trying to pressure us into making a decision. Let's say no. Anyone can yes to one hundred thousand Reichsmarks, but how many can say no?"

Arnold agreed, and they refused the offer.

Years later, they would say that this difficult decision saved their lives: "If we had taken the money, we would have bought a beautiful home, filled it with lovely furniture and, like so many others, would not have been able to leave immediately when Hitler came to power." Instead, the Schoenbergs left Germany at the earliest opportunity, settled in California, and lived many more productive years.

In this story I see a lesson that involves both courage and discernment. Let me recap the scenario: A door opens. The opportunity doesn't seem to be overladen with moral issues in which one choice is obviously right and the other wrong. Actually the opportunity looks great—almost too good to be true. Why would anyone not say yes?

But one's heart says that something is not right here. It's not just your natural resistance or fear of "the new." It's an underlying lack of peace that says no—stop.

Not every open door is meant to be walked through. Sometimes God wants us to have the courage to say no—to follow His leading and trust Him for an open door with His blessing.

Father, open my spiritual ears so I can hear the voice of Your Spirit whispering to me. Give me courage as I make my daily decisions. If I hear Your "Stop!" give me the confidence I need in order to act on that word without hesitation.

Pier Francesco Cavalli (1602–1676)

Courage to Chart a New Course

Sing to him a new song; play skillfully, and shout for joy.
—Psalm 33:3

Cavalli. Is it a type of pasta?

Wrong. Pier Franceso Cavalli was a seventeenth-century Venetian composer whose works are seldom performed or studied. Today his name is unknown even to many musicians, but in his day, Cavalli was a very important Italian composer. In his seventy-three years he wrote forty-two operas, though most are now forgotten. As a composer, Cavalli never had the talent to create dozens of masterpieces that would endure the test of time.

Yet Cavalli's musical influence has had a dramatic effect on hundreds of composers to this day—including *all* the great opera creators—even though many of the masters may have never heard of him!

How did this surreptitious influence take place? Cavalli was writing operas when that genre was still in its early stages. In those days, an opera included many undramatic halts between songs; in these pauses the singers intoned long, boring texts to tell the story itself. Composers employed a declamatory technique known as *recitative*, in which the singer would quickly—often on the same note with minimal accompaniment—sing line after line of the story. These sections were often considered so musically unimportant that patrons would excuse themselves, go outside, and wait until the time for their favorite songs!

Cavalli was one of the first composers to see the folly of this. He began to write a new kind of opera—a dramatic style from start to finish. This style might seem obvious today, but at the time it was a novelty—a new approach that took innovative insight. Cavalli was a man who wasn't stopped by the brick wall that kills so many good ideas: "But we've never done it like this before."

One mark of a creative person is the ability to see new ways of doing things. Creative, *courageous* persons can act on the idea and get beyond the internal or external resistance to something that's different.

That mix of creativity and courage can influence generations. Not everyone can be a Mozart or a Verdi, but each of us has good ideas that can help others. Although Cavalli himself did not possess the brilliance to create history's greatest operas, composers for centuries will be in his debt.

In your work, your artistic pursuits, your ministry, even your household, do you see a "better way" of doing things? Do you have a vision for something new but are afraid you'll get ridiculed because it's too "unusual"?

Go for it. Call it your Cavalli courage and transform a boring recitative into a dramatic production.

Father, You've blessed me with ideas that I sense are worth pursuing, but it's going to take some courage to get things moving in a new direction. Give me wisdom to chart a new course that may be hard for me and for those around me. Give me the joy that comes when You lead me out of a dark rut into the light, fresh air.

Zoltán Kodály (1882–1967)

Courage to Come Forth As Gold

But he knows the way that I take; when he has tested me, I will come forth as gold.
—Job 23:10

Zoltán Kodály was not the "hero-type." As a professor and musicologist, he worked quietly at a desk. Kodály loved his native Hungary and held strong beliefs about composers' retaining connections with their ancestral roots. He spent hours studying and cataloging Hungarian folk music. This native influence found its way into Kodály's own music in acclaimed works such as the *Hary Janos* suite for orchestra and the colossal choral work *Psalmus Hungaricus.*

But the celebrity status that Kodály enjoyed as a Hungarian composer was tempered by the affliction his country endured during World War II. Under Nazi occupation, he was ordered to divorce his Jewish wife. Kodály refused and went further in his protests by joining "the underground" in its efforts to find sanctuary for fleeing Jews.

When caught in his covert activities, he was questioned near a concentration camp and threatened with torture. No. He still refused to cooperate and give the enemy any information. Concerned about the repercussions of their harming or imprisoning such a notable national, the Nazis finally released him.

This quiet professor walked through the refining fire of suffering and emerged with strength and purpose. The war left this great man penniless but as creative as ever. In 1946 he

remarked, "There is no greater stimulus for artistic work than suffering."

In a number of Scripture passages, God's people are compared with gold; this beautiful gold is refined and perfected through fire. God may lead us through the fire of adversity, hardship, and suffering, to bring us closer to the perfection He envisions for us.

The Bible repeatedly promises God's everpresence in times of trouble. Whether we "feel" His presence or not, He is there, extending His love and grace.

If you are hurting, remember and claim this promise for yourself:

> When you pass through the waters, I will be with you; and when you pass through the rivers, they will not sweep over you. When you walk through the fire, you will not be burned; the flames will not set you ablaze (Isa. 43:2).

Resting in that promise, try to look beyond your pain (the fire) for evidence of refined gold. Has the trial inspired you to some new creative work? Has it made you more sensitive to the needs of others? More aware of your reliance on God and His grace?

Father, when I feel as if the fire will consume me, help me to look for You walking with me in the fire. Then help me look beyond the fire—to discover the golden wonders of Your redemptive work.

Thomas Ken (1637–1710)

Courage Fueled by Praise

Glorify the LORD with me; let us exalt his name together. I sought the LORD, and he answered me; he delivered me from all my fears.
—Psalm 34:3–4

Across the world many churches sing one particular song of praise every Sunday. In just a few lines it summarizes great themes of the Christian faith.

Praise God, from whom all blessings flow;
Praise him, all creatures here below;
Praise him above, ye heavenly host;
Praise Father, Son, and Holy Ghost.

Who wrote these words?

Thomas Ken was a prominent Anglican clergyman in an age when the English nobility was not known for its saintliness. More than once he felt compelled to remain true to his conscience, even when that meant disagreeing with or opposing the king.

As royal chaplain to King Charles II, Ken received the news that the king was coming to Ken's town of Winchester. What's more, King Charles insisted that during this visit the king's mistress would stay in Ken's house.

Hearing this news, Ken was dismayed. He did not wish to be disloyal to his monarch, but the king's mistress was *not* going to sleep in the chaplain's home. What to do? Ken quickly began major repairs on his house, even having workmen remove his entire roof. When Charles and his attendants

arrived, Ken apologized and pointed to the bare beams. The king, only slightly disgruntled, made other plans.

In that instance a confrontation was avoided by some quick thinking and maneuvering, but when James II became king in 1688, Thomas Ken's convictions would cost his freedom. Now a bishop, Ken and several others refused to endorse or enforce the king's Declaration of Indulgence. James threw the bishops in prison in the Tower of London. Eventually tried and acquitted, Ken returned home to a quiet retirement.

These stories mark a man of courage who was unwilling to compromise his conscience. He was also a man of wisdom, knowing that there is not one plan of action that works in every situation. Sometimes it may be appropriate to quickly maneuver ourselves away from compromising situations. At other times we may need to take a stand and firmly say, "No. That is wrong."

I like to think that Ken's courage was fueled by the praise that was on his lips. You see, years before these royal encounters, he'd written the lines we now know as the doxology. He wrote them as a "last verse" for several hymns sung at the Winchester Cathedral. Note that I said "several" hymns. He didn't want the words sung just once. He wanted this praise to be repeated at services in the morning, afternoon, and night.

Do you feel in need of courage to take a stand? You can find that courage in an intimate relationship with the true King "from whom all blessings flow." Praise Him for His blessings. Look to Him to lift your fear and empower you to act on what is right.

Father, I—one of Your creatures here below—praise You—from whom all blessings flow. Turn my praise into courage to do what is right.

Arthur Honegger (1892–1955)

Courage to Resist Evil

Have nothing to do with the fruitless deeds of darkness, but rather expose them.
—Ephesians 5:11

Frenchman Arthur Honegger was one of Europe's most interesting twentieth-century composers. His music ranges from the powerful choruses of the oratorio *King David*, to the innovative rhythms and dissonances of *Pacific 231,* a musical depiction of an enormous train in motion.

Though Honegger could have fled Paris when the Nazis invaded France, he chose to remain with his suffering countrymen. One might say that he laid low, becoming a virtual hermit in his studio, but that doesn't mean he was inactive; you see, Honegger was an integral link in the French resistance.

Suspicion was inevitable, especially as Honegger repeatedly refused flattering invitations to conduct concerts in Germany. Risking his career? Yes—maybe his life.

As for his work, he kept at it, composing some of his greatest works in the midst of the danger. By God's grace, Honegger was never arrested. One of his compositions, appropriately entitled *Chant de Liberation*, was triumphantly performed just two months after the liberation of Paris.

In various ways, Scripture tells us to resist evil. The most notable passage might be James 4:7: "Resist the devil, and he will flee from you." Then there is 1 Peter 5:8–9: "Your enemy the devil prowls around like a roaring lion looking for someone to devour. Resist him, standing firm in the faith . . ."

Arthur Honegger quietly resisted societal evil, but some-

times we are called to make the courageous choice to resist evil on a more personal level. It might mean separating ourselves from certain people and activities. Separating ourselves from compromise. Sometimes it is simply resisting a besetting temptation.

Peter admonishes: "Dear friends, I urge you, as aliens and strangers in the world, to abstain from sinful desires, which war against your soul" (1 Peter 2:11).

For you—today—what does resisting evil mean? Remember this additional verse on temptation—full of promise that there is a way out: "No temptation has seized you except what is common to man. And God is faithful; he will not let you be tempted beyond what you can bear. But when you are tempted, he will also provide a way out so that you can stand up under it" (1 Cor. 10:13). We have a God who is always willing to help His children who sincerely want to do His will.

Father, it takes such courage to resist evil. Give me the strength to resist and the desire to walk with You.

Modest Mussorgsky (1839–1881)

Courage to Fight Injustice

Act with courage, and may the LORD be with those who do well.
—2 Chronicles 19:11

After years of difficult composition, rejection, and revision, Modest Mussorgsky premiered his opera *Boris Godunov* on January 8, 1874, in the Imperial Theater in St. Petersburg. It was to be his masterpiece, but composing the work had taken its toll; a poorly paid clerk in Russia's Ministry of Transport, he composed "on the side." There were just too few hours in a day, and now his health was failing.

He faced other stresses: Composing this particular opera took a great deal of courage. Instead of another opera glorifying the extravagance of the nobility, this work would stand up for the average Russian—poor, oppressed, and without hope. It epitomized the intensity of the Russian people's soul.

Mussorgsky's libretto was based on Pushkin's drama with the unwieldy but descriptive title: "The Comedy of the Distress of the Muscovite State and of the Tzar Boris."

How was the czarist regime going to view such an opera premiere? In Mussorgsky's day siding against the czar and with the common rabble could result in persecution, exile, or even death. The composer knew what he was up against, but he refused to cower to the unjust power of the regime.

Sure enough, the czar heard about the unorthodox opera. After only twenty-five performances, the work was banned. Fortunately, Mussorgsky did not have to pay for his convictions with his life. The opera was suppressed and he was

harassed, but a great statement had been proclaimed that would not be forgotten by the Russian people.

Now we see *Boris Godunov* as a glorious addition to the standard opera repertoire. But as Mussorgsky struggled to get the music and words on paper, he had good reason to fear for his work's reception. Would it cost him his freedom or his life? He was certainly afraid, but he did not succumb to that fear. Through his art, he bravely confronted the injustice of his day.

Courage is not an absence of fear. Feeling fear need not churn up the additional negative emotion of guilt. Courage means refusing to allow that fear to stop or paralyze us. It means *stepping out* and taking the action demanded of us—no matter how terrifying.

If you feel that God has asked you to do something but you hold back in fear, turn to the Lord for an infusion of *His* strength. He will give you grace to face the task. Then take action. Never forget the Lord's stirring words to Joshua, facing a frightening assignment: "Have I not commanded you? Be strong and courageous. Do not be terrified; do not be discouraged, for the LORD your God will be with you wherever you go" (Josh. 1:9).

Father, sometimes I see injustice and I am horrified—horrified but also afraid to step out and do something that might change the situation. I'm challenged by the story of Modest Mussorgsky who found the time and energy and courage to do what he could to make a difference in his world. I look to You for that kind of spirit-strength.

Part Eight

Musical Grace Notes

Grace to Receive, Grace to Give

Let your conversation be always full of grace,
seasoned with salt, so that you may know how to answer everyone.
—Colossians 4:6

Follow the teachings of our Lord Jesus Christ
and walk in his footsteps.
Francis of Assisi

Franz Liszt and Friends

Franz Liszt (1811–1886)

Forgiving Grace

A man's wisdom gives him patience; it is to his glory to overlook an offense.
—Proverbs 19:11

I've said it before in these pages. I'll say it again: In his day Franz Liszt was famed as the world's finest pianist—number one in his class.

Well behind him in reputation, many lesser pianists attempted to scratch out careers, sometimes stooping to unscrupulous methods to capture attention. One young woman in this group (her name has mercifully been forgotten) concocted a notorious whopper to attract a larger audience. For a recital in Berlin, she advertised extensively that she was a "pupil of Liszt" (whom she had never even met!).

She assumed she could get away with this. Who would know her secret? And surely Liszt would never find out.

Imagine her horror when, on the very morning of her publicized performance, the newspapers announced that Liszt himself had just arrived in Berlin. What could she do now? Her duplicity would be publicly exposed, and she would be disgraced. After wrestling with remorse, she decided to go to Liszt and confess her misdeed.

Begging for an interview at his hotel, the woman entered his suite in trepidation, fearing the master's wrath for such a disrespectful offense. With many tears she confessed—and waited, expecting to be banished from his presence.

Far from showing fury, the great Liszt attended her thoughtfully as he worked through an idea in his head.

The woman listened incredulously as Liszt quietly asked her the name of each piece on her program. Selecting one, he asked her to sit at his piano and play it for him.

She began. Liszt listened and eventually interrupted with several hints about how to perform the composition. Then he smiled, and with a pat on the cheek, he dismissed her: "Now, my dear, you may call yourself a pupil of Liszt."

By his actions he went beyond forgiveness. He helped her save face.

That wiser and humbler woman left the hotel, graced with a Christlike gesture of clemency. To an adulterous woman Jesus said, "Neither do I condemn you . . . Go now and leave your life of sin" (John 8:11).

When someone shows you disrespect or more blatantly "sins against" you, how do you react? Like Liszt? Like Christ? Can you even contemplate the possibility of leaving "vengeance" to God and repaying an offender with kindness?

"Be kind and compassionate to one another, forgiving each other, just as in Christ God forgave you" (Eph. 4:32).

Father, I need Your grace in this area. It is easier for me to hold grudges than to forgive and move on. Help me to have Your forgiving nature and a heart of compassion. You have forgiven me so much; now let me extend this forgiveness and love toward others.

Antonin Dvořák (1841–1904)

Gospel Grace

The first thing Andrew did was to find his brother Simon and tell him, "We have found the Messiah," (that is, the Christ). Then he brought Simon to Jesus.
—John 1:41–42

Johannes Brahms was among Antonin Dvořák's dearest friends and most enthusiastic supporters. Brahms convinced his publisher to distribute Dvořák's music, and he influenced musicians throughout Europe to play the young composer's works. The bachelor Brahms even financially helped Dvořák's struggling family.

While very grateful for Brahms's support, Dvořák grieved over his mentor's lapses of faith or spiritual confusion. Brahms had read many speculations by non-Christian philosophers, and his spiritual life was sometimes marked by periods of doubt and lack of assurance. Brahms was not an agnostic, but when the two men discussed religion Dvořák often walked away distressed over what he had heard.

History records this comment made by someone who had heard the two discuss religion at length: "On the way back to the hotel, Dvořák was more than usually silent. At last after some considerable time he exclaimed with some emotion, 'Such a man, such a soul—and he doesn't believe in anything; he doesn't believe in anything!'"

There was anguish in Dvořák's remark—anguish for his friend's soul. Dvořák, known as a man of prayer, certainly prayed fervently for Brahms and his relationship with God.

What about your friends, colleagues, and family? Do you take the time to share your faith with them? Do you encourage them spiritually? Pray for them? Have they heard a clear

presentation of the gospel message? Or are you afraid of what they might think of you?

Rather than try to save the whole world, why not select one specific person you know who needs the Lord. Ask God to give you a serious prayer burden for that individual. Commit to pray daily for his or her salvation. Ask the Lord to open up natural opportunities for you to share God's love and message with this person. Ask Him to fulfill the words of Paul in your life and witness: "Be wise in the way you act toward outsiders; make the most of every opportunity. Let your conversation be always full of grace, seasoned with salt, so that you may know how to answer everyone" (Col. 4:5–6).

Father, I pray for (name). *I pray for his salvation, that he will see his need for a Savior. Lord, help him to know of the love and forgiveness You have to offer. Please help me to be a steadfast witness for You. Give me opportunities to share, give me Your words to speak, give me boldness and sensitivity to be Your ambassador to those around me.*

Francis of Assisi (1182–1226)

An Instrument of Grace

Blessed is he who is kind to the needy.
—Proverbs 14:21

The fiery summer sun grilled the Italian countryside. For the sick man in the primitive hut there was no escaping the oppressive heat. He was too sick to notice the field mice scrambling near him in the straw. Indeed, his illness had temporarily blinded him. In the solitary dark, he spent hours thinking back over his life's work for God.

The man's name was Francesco Bernardone, but history would remember him as Francis of Assisi. After coming to Christ as a young man, Francis believed that he heard God's voice, commanding him to "rebuild my church." Having no co-workers at the beginning, he took God's Word literally and began singlehandedly to repair the ruins of a chapel near Assisi.

Seeing how the pursuit of riches had dampened the faith of many fellow Christians, Francis renounced all worldly goods and devoted himself to two activities: preaching repentance and caring for the poor.

A story is told of his walking in the country and coming upon a leper who, at first glance, was repulsive to look at. But when the Lord opened his eyes to see the sick man as someone deeply loved by God, Francis quickly embraced and helped the leper.

As Francis' devout reputation spread, other young men joined him. He taught them how to care for the sick, the lepers,

the outcasts; he exhorted them to preach the gospel to everyone. The first rule for his followers was "to follow the teachings of our Lord Jesus Christ and to walk in his footsteps."

The brotherhood spread rapidly and Francis laid out great missionary plans. He and his followers took the gospel to the Muslims in Morocco, and later to Syria and Egypt—where Francis boldly shared Christ's message with the sultan himself.

Yet Francis's evangelistic zeal abroad did not hinder his continual care toward those at home. His ministry reached thousands of Italian peasants and orphans. He taught the friars to show God's love to every person, regardless of status. Those close to him testified of Francis's great tenderness toward all, even animals and birds.

Now, as he lay in the summer heat, he faced the closing of a chapter in his life's work. The year before, in 1222, the Franciscan Order had been placed in other hands. A new administration was already making ministry changes that disturbed him, but he submitted humbly and did not invite division. His life was Christ's; he would entrust the future of his work to the Lord.

Within that wretched hut, a joy that was characteristic of Francis's work began to stir his soul. And during this time of illness, he wrote a song of praise that remains a favorite to this day:

All creatures of our God and King,
Lift up your voice and with us sing
Alleluia!
Thou burning sun with golden beam,
Thou silver moon with softer beam,
O praise him, Alleluia!

The hands-on ministry of Francis of Assisi is an example for each of us. God calls us to love the unlovable and to care for those who cannot repay the kindness.

This week you may encounter someone you don't naturally "take to." His or her personality may grate on your nerves. Her physical hygiene may be deplorable. His sickness may be physically repulsive. Think of Francis of Assisi and his grace to reach out with God's love. And remember Christ's words: "I tell you the truth, whatever you did for one of the least of these brothers of mine, you did for me" (Matt. 25:40).

Lord,
Make me an instrument of Your peace.
Where there is hatred, let me sow love;
Where there is injury, pardon;
Where there is doubt, faith;
Where there is despair, hope;
Where there is darkness, light, and
Where there is sadness, joy.
O divine Master,
Grant that I may not so much
Seek to be consoled as to console;
To be understood as to understand;
To be loved as to love;
For it is in giving that we receive;
It is in pardoning that we are pardoned; and
It is in dying that we are born to eternal life.

Lord, like Francis—and with the sun and moon above—I praise You. I thank You for Your love—a love that reached down to earth to become one of us. Give me the vision that sees others with Your eyes of love. Give me the desire and grace to reach out and be love for others.

Rise in the presence of the aged, show respect for the elderly and revere your God.
—Leviticus 19:32

Johann Sebastian Bach (1685–1750)

Ageless Grace

This may be a story of Prussia's King Frederick the Great (1712–1786) more than of Bach. You can be the judge.

When Frederick wasn't fighting battles, he was playing music. He was an accomplished flutist and composed music himself. Every evening featured a private concert in the palace, usually with the king performing flute concertos. Besides his own playing, Frederick had the largest musical court in Europe.

One of J. S. Bach's many sons, Carl Philipp Emanuel Bach, was employed in Frederick's musical entourage. In 1747 the king, having heard about the elder Bach's accomplishments, invited "Old Bach," as he was called, to the palace.

J. S. Bach was then in his sixties and would die within a few years, but he made the journey with his son, arriving at the palace early one evening just as the king was preparing to perform.

Notified of the guest's arrival, Frederick quickly set aside his flute, announcing to the orchestra, "Gentlemen, Old Bach has come." Still in his traveling clothes, Bach was immediately brought before the king, who treated him with the greatest of royal respect.

Frederick insisted that Bach play on each of the many palace keyboard instruments; the musicians followed from room to room as the old man improvised skillfully. Frederick

would give Bach musical themes, on which Bach would instantly compose harmony and variations—to the king's delight. Pushing Bach to the limit, the king asked for a huge, six-part fugue, which Bach improvised with full harmony before the astonished assembly. "Old Bach"—generally considered behind the times—was again the hero of the day.

We still enjoy some of the fruit of this historic meeting. After Bach returned home, he wrote down that six-part fugue. He added more material to it, leaving for posterity one of his late great works, *The Musical Offering*. This fascinating composition, dedicated to Frederick the Great, is still frequently heard today.

Back to Frederick. I like the way this man treated the "Old Bach," whose baroque music was out of fashion. The future was with rococo style. Who wanted or needed to pay tribute to a "has-been"? I can imagine young musicians in his court rolling their eyes at the sight of the elderly musician's entrance in a black cantor's gown.

The king knew the importance of having and showing respect for the aged, and he was wise enough to want to learn from his elders.

When the day comes that I am considered a "has-been," I hope a younger generation will show me the respect that is due any older person, as evident in Leviticus 19:32: "Rise in the presence of the aged, show respect for the elderly."

That is a respect I want to show the men and women who are a generation or two older than I.

Won't you join me—doing unto elders as we hope the younger will do unto us?

Father, let me be a blessing to the seniors around me, showing respect and love—and learning from the wisdom they have received from You.

Remembering the words the Lord Jesus himself said: "It is more blessed to give than to receive."
—Acts 20:35

CHARLES IVES (1874–1954)

A Giving Grace

Charles Ives was offered both wealth and renown, but he chose neither. He simply had more important things to do—such as giving his life away to others.

As a musician, Charles Ives, the first great American composer, was virtually unknown in his lifetime. In some circles he was known as cofounder of a very successful insurance company.

"Off the job" at home, the composer emerged, toiling over his innovative music year after unacclaimed year, producing magnificent chamber music, songs, symphonies, and piano repertoire.

Ives's steadfast Christian faith was an integral part of his compositional process. He set to music numerous psalms, and dozens of gospel and hymn melodies run through his work, framed in incredibly unusual settings. From chamber music to huge orchestral scores, he used more than fifty different hymn tunes, including "Jesus, Lover of My Soul," "Just As I Am Without One Plea," and "What a Friend We Have in Jesus."

In his later years, Ives's genius was at last acknowledged by the musical community, yet he did his best to hide from this fame, seldom appearing at performances of his music. Because his works were so complex, some were not performed and appreciated for years; his *Third Symphony* was first performed thirty-five years after it was composed—and then it received a Pulitzer Prize.

His unassuming generosity toward fellow musicians was common knowledge. Ives gave away his Pulitzer Prize money, remarking, "Prizes are for boys. I'm grown up!" He was simply not interested in worldly ambitions. Once when his secretary requested an autograph for her son, he jokingly answered, "The only time you get my autograph is on a check."

Knowing only his music, one would be awed by his revolutionary innovations. Knowing the man, one is aware of a down-to-earth, God-loving, people-loving human being.

Ives could have easily been a millionaire from his prosperous insurance business, yet he accepted only the funds required to meet his family's needs. Motivated by this same ideal, he refused payment for his compositions. Staunchly believing that his works should be available to all, he refused to copyright his music. He finally acquiesced but with the stipulation that the earnings be used to help publish the works of younger composers.

Ordinary, needy people held a special place in the heart of Charles Ives. The family housekeeper for seventeen years fondly remembered his friendly jokes, his playing hymns on the piano, his help in washing the dishes. His nephew recalled, "He was always interested in the underprivileged and physically handicapped. He had a sincere interest in anyone who needed help."

I wish I could have known this man of great talent and faith who took a sacrificial and sincere interest in others. Through his business and later through his art, he could have had whatever he wanted in terms of money and fame, but he chose instead to give of his resources and of himself on behalf of others.

He knew what was important. Do you and I know?

Father, forgive my selfishness and give me a caring heart.

Carry each other's burdens, and in this way you will fulfill the law of Christ.
—Galatians 6:2

GIUSEPPE VERDI (1813–1901)

Grace Through Grief

Of all the tragic or comic operas composed by Giuseppe Verdi, none could ever portray the intensity of his emotion as a young man in 1840: In April, his baby boy fell ill and died in his mother's arms. A few days later, a daughter also became sick and died. Then in June, Verdi's wife developed an acute "brain fever"—a third coffin was carried from his house.

He later remembered, "I was alone!—alone! In the space of about two months three loved ones had disappeared forever."

Though overwhelmed with such grief, Verdi was still under contract to compose, one commission being for a comic opera! When that work failed miserably, being withdrawn after only one performance, Verdi wanted to give up everything. He wrote the impresario Merelli, asking to be released from all future work.

We know little about this Merelli, but his love for and belief in the young composer saved Verdi's career—if not his life. Instead of giving up on the still-unknown musician, Merelli told him, "Listen, Verdi, I cannot make you write by force. My confidence in you has not lessened." Though not forcing a commission, he simply promised to stage any future opera that Verdi might compose.

A wise man, Merelli knew that starting work on a worthwhile project is often the way out of our troubles. Some time

later he met Verdi and tactfully suggested that he write another opera. When Verdi refused, Merelli handed him a libretto. You can imagine the scene: *Here—I thought you might like to read this.*

Verdi politely took the package home and reluctantly opened the manuscript: "I ran through the verses, and was much impressed by them, the more so that they formed almost a paraphrase of the Bible, the reading of which was always dear to me." Titled *Nabucco* or "Nebuchadnezzar," the libretto recounted the Babylonian captivity of the Jews, Nebuchadnezzar's madness and recovery, and the king's subsequent conversion to faith in Jehovah.

With the encouragement of Merelli, Verdi overcame his despair and set to work. In his own words, "One day one verse, one day another, one time a note, another time a phrase, and little by little the opera was written." It was one of his first great successes and is a beautiful piece of today's opera repertoire.

Merelli, a very busy man, could have easily dismissed the young, unknown composer plagued with ill-fortune. Instead, his care and encouragement saved Verdi from giving up. Without such kindness, Verdi's name would not be known today, because his greatest works were all written after 1840. Merelli was a true friend when Verdi most needed one.

Do you know someone grieving a loss—a relationship, a job, a familiar place or routine—who might need an extra dose of personal care? What can you do to lighten that person's load? At one stage your role might be to listen or to refuse to give up on him. Then at some point an encourager's role might be to suggest some worthwhile activity that God might use to widen the person's vision or involvement with the world.

I challenge you with Paul's counsel: "We who are strong ought to bear with the failings of the weak and not to please ourselves. Each of us should please his neighbor for his good, to build him up" (Rom. 15:1–2).

Lord, when I feel so weak that I can hardly face another day, please send me friends who will stick by. Your Word reminds me of this reality—the one who wants friends should be a friend. So today help me to be a friend to someone facing a loss. May Your care become my care.

JOHN NEWTON (1725–1807)

What's So Amazing About Grace?

I thank Christ Jesus our Lord, who has given me strength, that he considered me faithful, appointing me to his service. Even though I was once a blasphemer and a persecutor and a violent man, I was shown mercy because I acted in ignorance and unbelief.
—1 Timothy 1:12–13

The ship pitched and tossed in the open sea, yet the motion and the sea spray did not distract the sailor intent on his reading. He had recently been given the classic by Thomas à Kempis, *The Imitation of Christ.* He was both fascinated and convicted by the words on the damp pages. The author kept emphasizing the immeasurable grace of God, freely extended to all.

Though still in his twenties, John Newton had been at sea since early adolescence. He had long since abandoned his Christian upbringing. As a sailor, and later a slave trader, he took great pleasure in shocking people with his lecherous profanity. He seemed as far from God as one side of the ocean is from the other.

The night after finishing *The Imitation of Christ*, Newton's old ship hit a storm that convinced everyone aboard that the waterlogged craft was doomed. In the midst of the tempest, Newton cried out to God, who saved the ship—and transformed Newton's life.

A few years later, Newton left the sea. Eventually he felt called to full-time pastoral ministry. Without a university education, he crossed many hurdles before being ordained; at the age of forty, he took his first pastorate in the little English village of Olney.

Newton had a remarkable gift of communicating the truth of the Bible, both in his speaking and his writing. One day, wanting to compose a hymn for his congregation, he thought back over his debauched slave-trading years. He slowly wrote what was more than a simple hymn; it was the story of his own life:

Amazing grace! How sweet the sound,
That saved a wretch like me!
I once was lost, but now am found,
Was blind, but now I see.

The grace of God that had saved such a wretched sinner as himself would always figure predominantly in Newton's preaching, continuing through a pastorate in London, where he preached until he died, an octogenarian.

Think for a moment. Ponder the most cruel, heartless person in history. Now consider that Jesus Christ died for that person. On some lesser scale, you may know someone who seems simply *too* selfish or wicked to be saved. In your mind a Christian witness to this person seems fruitless; he or she seems impenetrable and imperturbable.

Then consider John Newton, the iniquitous slaver who become one of England's great preachers, whose hymn is probably the best-known gospel song in America today.

Finally, contemplate the words of Titus 2:11: "The grace of God that brings salvation has appeared to *all* men." God never gives up on anyone, and neither should we.

Father, thank You for Your amazing grace that has reached down to me. I thank You for a grace that can transform the vilest of hearts, a grace that doesn't give up. Forgive me when I give up on brothers and sisters whom You love. And help me to be an instrument of Your grace, leading others into Your open arms.

Part Nine

Musical Devotion

Becoming Passionate for God

I consider my life worth nothing to me, if only I may finish the race and complete the task the Lord Jesus has given me —the task of testifying to the Gospel of God's grace.

Acts 20:24

God is ever before my eyes. I realize His omnipotence and I fear His anger; but I also recognize His love, His compassion, and His tenderness towards His creatures. He will never forsake His own. If it is according to His will, so let it be according to mine. Thus all will be well and I must needs be happy and contented.

—Wolfgang Amadeus Mozart

Frédéric Chopin

Repent, then, and turn to God, so that your sins may be wiped out, that times of refreshing may come from the Lord.
—Acts 3:19

Frédéric Chopin (1810–1849)

Coming Home to Jesus

Pianist-composer Frédéric Chopin, raised by loving, devoutly Christian parents, grew up having a sincere faith and love for the Lord. After he had left Poland for a musical career in Western Europe, his parents wrote him constantly, assuring him, "Your old father and mother live only for you and pray God every day to bless and keep you."

But far from home, amid a hundred new and enticing influences, the young musician succumbed to the temptations of the high life. Giving one successful concert after another, he became the darling of the Paris salons. He was simply not spiritually equipped to handle the fast track to fame; news of his unhealthy relationships, including a long liaison with the woman who wrote novels under the name "George Sands," grieved his distant parents—who kept praying.

And God heard their fervent prayers. Chopin eventually turned away from Sands and many other questionable influences. Throughout his European travels Chopin had never forgotten his upbringing in Poland, and toward the end of his life, cut short by pulmonary tuberculosis, he sent for Abbe Jelowicki, a boyhood friend who had entered the priesthood. This man's providential emergence saved Chopin's soul. After the two spent much time together, his old friend brought Chopin back to Christ.

Jelowicki remembered the jubilation that Chopin felt

after reaffirming his faith: "Patience, trust in God, even joyful confidence, never left him, in spite of all his sufferings, 'til his last breath. He was really happy, and called himself happy. In the midst of the sharpest sufferings he expressed only ecstatic joy, touching love of God, thankfulness that I had led him back to God."

At the age of thirty-nine, Chopin was on his deathbed. Jelowicki stayed with him through that last physical struggle, which lasted four days. When he sensed a final crisis, Chopin noticed the many people in the room with him. Turning to Jelowicki, he gasped, "Why do they not pray?" At these words, it is reported that all, Catholics and Protestants alike, fell on their knees in prayer.

With final gratitude for bringing him back to Christ, Chopin whispered to Jelowicki, "Without you I should have cracked like a pig." Taking a crucifix to his heart, Chopin gave his last joyful words: "Now I am at the source of Blessedness."

What joy God must have felt at the return of His son—like the exhilaration of the Prodigal Son's father: "We had to celebrate and be glad, because this brother of yours was dead and is alive again; he was lost and is found" (Luke 15:32).

Who are you in this story? Are you Chopin, who ecstatically returned to the Lord? Are you his parents, ardently praying for a straying loved one? Are you Jelowicki, who showed his concern by boldly sharing his faith and leading his friend to the Lord?

Whatever our part, let us never forget the supreme importance of one person's coming to Christ, for "There is rejoicing in the presence of the angels of God over one sinner who repents" (Luke 15:10).

Father, remind me that angels rejoiced in heaven when I came into Your fold. Help me to share the joy of Your salvation with others and remain steadfast in prayer for those who wander from Your side.

Wolfgang Amadeus Mozart (1756–1791)

Trusting in the Lord

Trust in the Lord with all your heart and lean not on your own understanding; in all your ways acknowledge him, and he will make your paths straight.
—Proverbs 3:5–6

"God is ever before my eyes. I realize His omnipotence and I fear His anger, but I also recognize His love, His compassion, and His tenderness towards His creatures. He will never forsake His own. If it is according to His will, so let it be according to mine. Thus all will be well and I must needs be happy and contented."

Who would guess that this portion of a letter was written by Wolfgang Amadeus Mozart? This is not the picture portrayed by a number of modern writers and movie-makers. The real Mozart was a very complex, spiritual man from whom we can learn a great deal.

The recollections of his friends and hundreds of his personal letters converge to reveal Mozart's true nature. An editor of his published letters, Friedrich Kerst, summarized, "Mozart was of a deeply religious nature. . . . Mozart stood toward God in a relationship of a child full of trust in his father."

Praise to God, statements of faith, and care for the spiritual lives of those around him punctuate his correspondence. Here's another sample: "It will greatly assist such happiness as I may have to hear that my dear father and my dear sister have submitted wholly to the will of God, with resignation and fortitude—and have put their whole confidence in Him, in the firm assurance that He orders all things for the best."

Although Mozart's life was tragically brief, he left us an

unprecedented musical legacy. He also left us a model of eighteenth-century faith. His incredible genius, acquired at such a very young age, may have tempted some to "lean on" their "own understanding."

Mozart's response to his own creative genius was to acknowledge an almighty God in control of His creation. In another letter he spoke of trusting God: "Let us put our trust in God and console ourselves with the thought that all is well, if it is in accordance with the will of the Almighty, as He knows best what is profitable and beneficial to our temporal happiness and our eternal salvation."

With such a trusting attitude, his talent was unhindered by the doubts and uncertainty that have plagued many artists. Mozart's faith left him free to use the talent given him, and it flowed from him in a never-ending stream of inspiration.

When frustrated or daunted by a problem or task before you, examine your heart. Are you trusting God? Are you believing that He knows best and is watching out for you? The confidence that comes from a simple and profound faith can enable you to overcome any obstacle in your path. During the Last Supper, Jesus told his disciples: "Do not let your hearts be troubled. Trust in God; trust also in me" (John 14:1).

Lord, I want to trust You unequivocally, as a child trusts his father. Forgive me when I doubt or am fearful for the future. Give me a heart of faith. I love You, Father.

Igor Stravinsky (1882–1971)

A Full-Sense Believer

Fear of man will prove to be a snare, but whoever trusts in the LORD is kept safe.
—Proverbs 29:25

Biographer Robert Craft one day accompanied composer Igor Stravinsky to his Russian Orthodox Church. I'm not sure what the man expected to see, but he reported this scene: Stravinsky quickly fell to the floor, prostrating himself before the altar. Then he knelt for two hours on a hard floor. After receiving Communion, he again prayed, touching his forehead to the floor.

It is a devotion that baffles most Westerners, because we prefer churches with carpeted aisles and padded seats, but maybe we can learn something from this man—one of the most important composers of the twentieth century.

Stravinsky was already world-famous in 1926 when he converted to Christianity at the age of forty-four. It is ironic that Stravinsky is best known as the composer of *Firebird*, *Petrushka*, and the *Rite of Spring*, the latter subtitled *Pictures of Pagan Russia*. These early ballets explore secular and even pagan subjects that give no hint to the personal faith in Christ that would later be central in his life and work.

When Stravinsky embraced the Christian faith, he was unashamed to speak of his convictions. The thought would never have crossed his mind to apologize for either his music or his Christian beliefs.

Soon after his conversion, Stravinsky was interviewed in Belgium. He declared, "The more one separates oneself from

the canons of the Christian church, the further one distances oneself from the truth. . . . Art is made of itself, and one cannot create upon a creation, even though we are ourselves graftings of Jesus Christ." The *Symphony of Psalms*, his next major work, he dedicated "to the glory of God."

Stravinsky [illegible] efinite ideas concerning God, music, and hi [illegible] ts. He proclaimed, "The church knew what th [illegible] new: Music praises God. Music is as well or bett [illegible] praise Him than the building of the church and all [illegible] tions; it is the church's greatest ornament." In a d [illegible] about church music, Robert Craft asked if one m [illegible] eliever to create sacred music. Stravinsky insisted, "[illegible] and not merely a believer in 'symbolic figures,' but in [illegible] n of the Lord, the person of the Devil, and the mirac [illegible] church."

As to his own compositional genius, Stravinsky asserted: "Only God can create. I make music from music." He also admi [illegible] my talents as God-given, and I have alw [illegible] for strength to use them."

[illegible] simply didn't let the opinion of others a [illegible] l for a higher audience. He once said, " [illegible] el I am concerned with is not CBS, in a [illegible] with the Big Book."

[illegible] d his creative imagination, establishing a [illegible] se for music composition. His ingenui [illegible] criticism, but he remained undaunted, tr [illegible] als. From the advanced rhythms of his early ballets to the neoclassic and serial works of his later life, he never copied the styles or devices of his fellow composers.

Sometimes it's good to ask oneself, "How strong are my convictions? How much pressure would it take for me to compromise my Christian standards? What am I willing to

do for my faith? Am I willing to kneel on a stone floor for hours at a time? Am I willing to uncompromisingly proclaim my faith in my Lord?"

Take courage from the faithful witness of Igor Stravinsky. One of his many biographers, Alexandre Tansman, called him "a believer, in the full sense of the term." Does the phrase describe you?

Father, I want to be a "believer, in the full sense of the term." Show me what that means in my world—today.

I have not departed from the commands of his lips; I have treasured the words of his mouth more than my daily bread.
—Job 23:12

Felix Mendelssohn-Bartholdy (1809–1847)

Loving God's Word

Scriptural texts have been the setting of thousands of musical compositions; through their music, countless composers have sought to exalt God's Word. One of the best examples is Felix Mendelssohn-Bartholdy, a Jew who converted to Christ at an early age.

The Bible was central to Mendelssohn's life—and the inspiration for a great deal of his music. He was convinced of the truth of Moses' words, "[These] are not just idle words for you—they are your life" (Deut. 32:47). He especially loved to set psalms to music.

Mendelssohn's biographer, Eric Werner, once wrote, "He was faithful to the Christian religion and took it seriously. Reverence, fear of God, the sense of praise, of gratitude, of bitter complaints and of pride in one's faith, all these lay in his personality. He had great respect for the Biblical Word." According to a good friend, "He felt that all faith must be based on Holy Writ."

When Mendelssohn set Scripture to music, he was very particular and precise about the wording. Mendelssohn once praised his librettist, "I am glad to learn that you are searching out the always heart-affecting sense of the Scriptural words." But when the text had been tampered with, Mendelssohn noted, "I have time after time had to restore the precise text of the Bible; it is the best in the end."

Mendelssohn's love of Scripture significantly affected his work. He composed considerable sacred music, notably his lovely psalm settings and the celebrated oratorios *Elijah* and *Saint Paul*. Listening to these works, one can sense the profound devotion the composer had for biblical texts.

And such devotion was evident in his strong reaction to others' ridicule of the Scriptures. His contemporary Hector Berlioz, a radical freethinker, said, "Mendelssohn believed firmly in his Lutheran religion, and I sometimes shocked him profoundly by laughing at the Bible." Such deplorable disrespect was too much for the devout Mendelssohn.

What is the place of the Bible in *our* lives? Is it something to read ceremoniously, perhaps once a week? Or is it truly "our daily bread," constant food for the soul?

Our relationship with the Lord, our love for our brothers and sisters, our desire to see all people know Christ—all of these and more are grounded in our bond with the Word of God.

May the psalmist's exclamation become ours: "Oh, how I love your law! I meditate on it all day long" (Ps. 119:97).

Father, make me hungry for Your Word. And as I read it, help me to learn to love Your words as they guide my path. Thank You for the glorious gift of the Bible, that we might have access to the Words of Life. Lord, "open my eyes that I may see wonderful things in your law" (Ps. 119:18).

We live by faith, not by sight.
—2 Corinthians 5:7

Ludwig van Beethoven (1770–1827)

The Evidence of Faith

March 26 marks the date of two important events in the life of Ludwig van Beethoven. On March 26, 1778, the seven-year-old boy gave his first public piano recital. And on this same date in 1827, Beethoven died. In the forty-nine years between those two events—against overwhelming obstacles—Beethoven gave the world some of the greatest music ever written.

Though he had many devoted friends, Beethoven lived a lonely life. He became incurably deaf, had no wife or family to encourage him, and possessed a genius so advanced that his music was not always appreciated in his time. Yet this man had a profound trust in God; he learned how to "live by faith, not by sight."

What evidence do we have of Beethoven's great faith?

He left behind diaries, letters, and "blank books" full of written conversations from his "silent" years. These recount the thoughts and speech of a man of faith. For example, "It was not a fortuitous meeting of chordal atoms that made the world; if order and beauty are reflected in the constitution of the universe, then there is a God."

We even find heartfelt and personal prayers:

"Therefore, calmly will I submit myself to all inconsistency and will place all my confidence in Your eternal goodness, O God! My soul shall rejoice in Thee, immutable Being. Be my rock, my light, forever my trust!"

In 1810 he told a friend how friendless he felt—except for the presence of God: "I have no friend; I must live by myself. I know, however, that God is nearer to me than others. I go without fear to Him, I have constantly recognized and understood Him."

Shortly before dying, he assured his brother that he was ready to make his peace with God, and on his deathbed he received Communion. Beethoven's friend, Anselm Huttenbrenner, was with the composer when he died, during a storm. Following a loud clap of thunder, Beethoven awoke from a coma. Huttenbrenner reported that Beethoven "opened his eyes, raised his right hand, his fist clenched, and looked upward for several seconds with a grave, threatening countenance, as if to say, 'I defy you, powers of evil! Away! God is with me!'"

Ask yourself this tough question: If a biographer should someday research my life, what tangible verifications of my faith would be found—from talking to my friends, from looking at my personal papers? What evidences of my faith are observable and noteworthy?

As Paul exhorted the Corinthians, "Examine yourselves to see whether you are in the faith" (2 Cor. 13:5). Let us daily examine our lives to see if there's evidence of faith in our Creator.

Father, help me to live daily by faith, and not by my natural sight. Help me to examine myself honestly and see if there is anything in me that is displeasing You. Let my faith be evident to all, that You may be glorified.

But I have stilled and quieted my soul.
—Psalm 131:2

Joseph Mohr (1792–1848)

Quieting Yourself Before the Lord

What to do?! It was December 24, 1818, and the pastor of Saint Nicholas Church in the Austrian village of Oberndorf was beside himself. He had spent weeks preparing a "perfect" Christmas Eve service, now suddenly everything had gone wrong.

The Reverend Joseph Mohr had just stumbled into every music director's nightmare: The church organ broke down, out of commission for the holiday service, and all the carefully chosen music had to be scrapped. Mohr had to come up with a suitable substitute quickly. Would he have to write a new song to carry the day?

In the midst of his panic, Mohr took the time to pray, asking for God's guidance. Following the psalmist's example, he "stilled and quieted" his soul before the Lord.

And in that stillness, a divine peace filled his heart. He tranquilly took paper and ink and wrote:

Silent Night, Holy Night,
All is calm, all is bright
Round yon virgin, mother and child,
Holy infant so tender and mild,
Sleep in heavenly peace,
Sleep in heavenly peace.

In a surprisingly short time, Mohr had composed a beautiful poem. He then asked his friend Franz Gruber (1787–1863)—the village schoolmaster and church organist—to set the words to music. That Christmas Eve, Oberndorf had a new song. The two men sang *Stille Nacht* as a duet, with Gruber accompanying on the guitar.

That might have been the end of an obscure story, but the organ still needed to be repaired! And God had further plans for the song *Silent Night*. When repairman Karl Mauracher arrived, he heard the song and asked for a copy. Mauracher then spread the carol throughout the Tyrol countryside as he repaired other instruments.

The song eventually got into the hands of the multitalented Stasser family of Zillertai. By day the family made gloves, which they sold at town fairs. While at the fairs, they drew a crowd by singing folk songs. At the Leipzig fair of 1831, the Stasser family created a "hit" performing *Stille Nacht*. In a few years it was known and sung all over the world—all because of a broken organ. Or rather, all because a man decided to turn from his anxiety and quiet himself before the Lord. Through this action, God was able to take a "predicament" and bring good from it.

If you are overwhelmed with "everything going wrong," try to follow Mohr's example. As the psalmist stilled and quieted his soul, seek the Lord for His heavenly peace, for His direction and inspiration that can turn a disaster into a blessed delight.

Father, I love You. Slow me down now, that I might know Your peace in the eye of the storm. Lord, help me to keep this peace as I walk out this day. Thank You for always working for my benefit. Praise Your holy name!

So you also, when you have done everything you were told to do, should say, "We are unworthy servants; we have only done our duty."
—Luke 17:10

Franz Joseph Haydn (1732–1809)
Giving God All the Glory

On March 27, 1808, Franz Joseph Haydn attended his last musical performance. The program featured his oratorio *The Creation*. He'd finished the massive work at age sixty-six, saying it had been composed to inspire "the adoration and worship of the Creator" and to put the listener "in a frame of mind where he is most susceptible to the kindness and omnipotence of the Creator."

Haydn recalled, "Never was I so devout as when I composed *The Creation*. I knelt down each day to pray to God to give me strength for my work." He told a friend, "When I was working on *The Creation,* I felt so impregnated with the Divine certainty that, before sitting down to the piano, I would quietly and confidently pray to God to grant me the talent that was needed to praise him worthily."

At this March 1808 performance of his triumphant oratorio, the composer was determined that God would get all the glory for his work. As the music faded and the audience applauded enthusiastically, Haydn lifted his hands and said, "Not from me—from there, above, comes everything."

Haydn always insisted that his talents were an unmerited gift from God—a gift that he should use to bless others. He told a group of musicians playing his *Creation*, "There are so few happy and contented people here below, sorrow and anxiety pursue them from everywhere; perhaps your work may, someday, become a spring from which the careworn may draw a few moments' rest and refreshment."

Haydn was well aware that he possessed talent at the genius level, but he always was quick to acknowledge the Author of this talent. Even his will begins: "In the Name of the Most Holy Trinity," and continues, "My soul I bequeath to its all-bountiful Creator."

It is all too easy to take the credit for the work we have done and to forget the Creator who enabled us to do the work. Our talents, our character, our knowledge, even our health are gifts from God, and to Him alone be all the glory.

Father, help me to see You—and praise You—as the Creator and Giver of life. Everything I have is from Your hand. You have given me so much. Today—and as I grow older and have more "success," help me to acknowledge You as the source of my gifts. Help me use the resources You have given me for Your glory alone.

Part Ten

Musical Inspiration

The Fire That Sparks the Creative Spirit

Fan into flame the gift of God.
2 Timothy 1:6

I did think I did see all Heaven before me,
and the great God Himself.
—George Frédéric Handel

Ludwig Van Beethoven

Ludwig Van Beethoven (1770–1827)

Inspired by God's Handiwork

Let the rivers clap their hands, let the mountains sing together for joy.
—Psalm 98:8

A young boy named Michael Krenn walked through the outskirts of Vienna, looking for the strange man who had employed his father as a servant. As the youth mounted a hill, he spied someone far away sitting by a brook. Yes, the boy knew that he had found his man.

Krenn later reported the bizarre scene: Jumping up from his seat on the ground, the eccentric "cried out, threw his hands about, walked fast, very slow, and then very fast, and then, all of a sudden, would stand quite still and write something in a kind of pocket book." The "character"—Ludwig van Beethoven—was composing in his favorite "studio"—the forests and fields of the great outdoors.

Nature was always one of Beethoven's greatest inspirations. For years his typical daily schedule included two long walks in the country, where he composed many of the masterpieces we still cherish. One of his good friends claimed that he had "never met anyone who so delighted in nature, or who so thoroughly enjoyed flowers, or clouds, or other natural objects. Nature was almost meat and drink to him; he seemed positively to exist on it."

Many diary excerpts describe Beethoven's love of nature. In 1812 he wrote: "Almighty One, in the woods I am blessed. Happy is everyone in the woods. Every tree speaks through Thee, O God! What glory is in the Woodland. On the

heights is peace—'Peace to serve Him.'" A note of 1814 confirmed that peace: "My miserable hearing does not trouble me here. In the country it seems as if every tree said to me: 'Holy, Holy!'—Who can give complete expression to the ecstasy of the woods!" And in 1818 he wrote, "Here I shall learn to know God and find a foretaste of heaven in His knowledge."

No matter what the weather, Beethoven would wander through the fields, sketchbook in hand, awaiting inspiration. One of his favorite sayings was, "The morning air has gold to spare." In one of his sketchbooks we find that he sang to himself the old hymn *God Alone Is Our Lord* "on the road in the evening, up and down among the mountains."

Perhaps the greatest example of nature's inspiration to Beethoven is his *Symphony No. 6*, the "Pastoral" Symphony. Each of its five exquisite movements has a descriptive programmatic title, such as "Cheerful Impressions Excited on Arriving in the Country," "By the Brook," "Peasants Merry Making," "Storm," "The Shepherd's Hymn, Gratitude and Thanksgiving After the Storm."

Many years after the premiere of the "Pastoral," Beethoven and his friend Anton Schindler walked into the country together. Leaning against an elm, the now-deaf composer asked if Schindler could hear any yellow hammers in the tree above. On receiving a negative answer, Beethoven recalled, "Here is where I wrote the 'Scene by the Brook,' while the yellow hammers were singing above me, and the quails, nightingales, and cuckoos called all around."

Even after he was deaf, Beethoven held onto the inspiration he had found in the beauty of God's world. His love of nature brought him closer to the Lord, for he was careful to worship the Creator rather than the creation.

Our Creator God delights in our delight of the creation He called "good." In our fast-paced world, we too often take nature for granted. When was the last time you were inspired by a sunset, a tree, a flower, a grand canyon—or a rolling brook?

The poetry of the Bible talks about nature itself praising God. "You will go out in joy and be led forth in peace; the mountains and hills will burst into song before you, and all the trees of the field will clap their hands" (Isa. 55:12).

Let's join the applause.

Father, I praise You for creating such an awesome world. Help me to catch a little of the Beethoven spirit—being inspired by the sights and sounds of Your handiwork.

Whoever welcomes a little child like this in my name welcomes me.
—Matthew 18:5

Antonin Dvořák (1841–1904)

Inspired by Family

In 1896 Antonin Dvořák began composing four pieces based on the "Garand" fairy tales of Karel Jaromir Erben. Such a project must have delighted this composer, who dearly loved his children and found musical inspiration within the love of his family.

By this time in his career he was internationally celebrated. He had traveled much of the world, yet he preferred the company of his family to that of the many dignitaries and fans who clamored for his appearance.

Dvořák loved to have his children near him whenever possible. A student once recalled: "His children were permitted to invade his studio at all times, even when the composer was at serious work. My daily lessons were usually taken with the accompaniment of grimacing boys and girls hidden behind articles of furniture or appearing at unexpected moments in doorways out of their father's sight."

Indeed, Dvořák was so approachable that, instead of seeking solitude, he often worked at the kitchen table. While his wife baked bread and his children played noisily throughout their home, Dvořák created some of his finest works. He certainly took his craft seriously, but he had such a love for his family that this famous composer never felt "too important" to stop for the smallest child.

Whenever Dvořák traveled abroad, he sent his children cheerful letters exhorting them to "pray fervently" and to attend church regularly. Even his greatest work, the beautiful *Stabat Mater*, was intimately related to his family. Dvořák based the composition on a poem by Jacopone di Todi that portrays the grief of Jesus' mother at her Son's death. The piece reflects Dvořák's own sadness at the loss of three of his children within a short time. This man with a father's heart was touched much more by his little ones than by the most adoring of fans.

Take a moment to reflect on your own family members. Do you generally find them inspiring or annoying? Do you wish you had more time for them, or more time to get your work done? Are your children in the way of your life or are they life itself?

Pause and pray for each member of your family. Ask God's blessing on them. Then ask Him to use them as your inspiration.

Focus your mind on that beautiful picture of our Lord Jesus, when He "called the children to him and said, 'Let the little children come to me, and do not hinder them, for the kingdom of God belongs to such as these'" (Luke 18:16).

Father, You are the most important Being in all the universe, yet You have time to hear every child's prayer. Help me to have that same perspective—to see my family members as You see them. Give me grace to "welcome the little children" as You would gladly receive them, and let their love inspire me in all that I do.

Be ready to do whatever is good.
—Titus 3:1

Ira D. Sankey (1840–1908)

Inspired by Need—and Faith

"Moody and Sankey" posters were still plastered all over the city. The great Dwight L. Moody and his musician partner Ira D. Sankey had just finished an evangelistic campaign in Glasgow, Scotland. Next stop? Edinburgh. Through their teamwork—powerful preaching and inspiring music—thousands were coming to Christ.

Before boarding the train to Edinburgh, Sankey bought a local newspaper. Finding little news of interest to an American, he was ready to discard the paper when he noticed a poem by Elizabeth Clephane, a name he didn't recognize. Reading the verse, titled "The Ninety and Nine," Sankey was struck to the heart. He even read the lines aloud before he clipped the poem and slipped it into his notebook.

Several days later with the Edinburgh crusade in high gear, Moody preached on "The Good Shepherd." Winding up his stirring sermon, he turned to Sankey and asked him to sing something appropriate to his topic.

Of course, today the music for a such big service would generally be planned well in advance. Not this time. The request took Sankey by surprise, and his mind went blank. In a frenzy, he flipped through his trusty music notebook but found nothing suitable to shepherds and sheep.

Ah—the poem he had found on the train! As thousands looked on, Sankey hurriedly pulled out the words of "The

Ninety and Nine." For such inspiring words there must be an inspiring tune waiting to be discovered. Sankey struck an A-flat chord on the organ, gulped, and set out on a compositional-improvisational quest. He found a lovely tune for these words:

> There were ninety and nine that safely lay
> In the shelter of the fold;
> But one was out on the hills away,
> Far off from the gates of gold;
> Away on the mountains wild and bare,
> Away from the tender Shepherd's care. . . .
>
> "Lord, Thou hast here Thy ninety and nine;
> Are they not enough for Thee?"
> But the Shepherd made answer: "This of mine
> Has wandered away from Me,
> And altho' the road be rough and steep,
> I go to the desert to find my sheep. . . ."
>
> "Lord, whence are those blood-drops all the way
> That mark out the mountain's track?"
> They were shed for one who had gone astray
> Ere the Shepherd could bring him back.
> "Lord, whence are Thy hands so rent and torn?"
> "They're pierced tonight by many a thorn. . . ."
>
> But all thro' the mountains, thunder-riv'n,
> And up from the rocky steep,
> There arose a glad cry to the gate of heav'n,
> "Rejoice! I have found my sheep!"
> And the angels echoed around the throne,
> "Rejoice, for the Lord brings back His own! . . ."

To his amazement and relief, he made it beautifully through the first stanza. The crowd was spellbound, having no idea, of course, that the music was being composed before their very eyes. He sang the second verse.

With the last note, Moody himself was visibly moved. That night hundreds were touched by the Spirit, committing their lives to the care of the Good Shepherd. Sankey later wrote down the song as he had improvised it, and even now it continues to reach out to wandering souls.

I've composed a great deal of music, from simple solos to complex concerti, and, believe me, there's nothing "simple" about getting it "right." Composing such a memorable piece on the spot before an audience would require both tremendous talent and extraordinary faith.

Many musicians would have panicked or balked and "run" in such a predicament, but risking public embarrassment (he didn't really know what would come out line by line), Sankey summoned his faith, worked with what he had at his disposal—inspiring lyrics—and rose to meet the need at hand.

No one likes to be put "on the spot." In the perfect scheme you would want ample time to prepare before attempting something that will be judged by others. But sometimes in His "higher" ways, God uses a pressing need to press an inspiring work out of us. He asks us to step out in faith and trust Him for inspiration.

Are you ready to step out in faith, as the Lord calls you?

"My righteous one will live by faith. And if he shrinks back, I will not be pleased with him. But we are not of those who shrink back and are destroyed, but of those who believe and are saved" (Heb. 10:38–39).

Lord, help me to be prepared to receive inspiration from Your Spirit that is meant to meet the needs before me. Give me ears to hear. Give me grace to walk by faith and to never shrink back when I hear Your call.

Bedřich Smetana (1824–1884)

Inspired by Love of Country

Then I said to them, "You see the trouble we are in: Jerusalem lies in ruins, and its gates have been burned with fire. Come, let us rebuild the wall of Jerusalem, and we will no longer be in disgrace."
—Nehemiah 2:17

Like Nehemiah of old, the first champion of Czech music, Bedřich Smetana, had a great desire to serve his country, at that time called Bohemia. A "born" musician, he had little opportunity for formal study. Even so he dreamed big plans; while still in his teens, he ambitiously wrote in his diary, "With God's help and grace, I will be a Mozart in composition and a Liszt in technique."

In 1843 he was finally able to study with his first competent teacher, Joseph Proksch of Prague. Smetana arrived in the capital, penniless, and was quickly disenchanted—not with his excellent teacher but with the sparse musical activity in Prague.

Many young men might simply have grumbled, but Smetana was determined to do something to remedy the situation. Again the young man had a dream. He would build a fine conservatory for the musical students of his country.

When his financial needs were met by a music teaching position with a local count, he began to make his dreams come true. In 1848 he secured official authorization to found a music school. The following year, Smetana married his lifelong sweetheart and became the official pianist to the former Emperor of Austria, who lived in Prague.

But Smetana's life fell apart when his four-year-old daughter died. He and his wife left Bohemia and settled in Sweden. A few years later he and his wife headed back home

to Bohemia, but Mrs. Smetena's death en route prompted Bedřich to stay in Sweden until 1861.

From the day Smetana finally returned to his beloved homeland, he gave his life to its musical world. He helped to create and administer the Philharmonic Society, rekindled the work of Prague's Provisional Theater, helped start the Society of Artists, and founded a dramatic school for the Bohemian Theater. Smetana became the director of a new school and a choral society; as a music critic he championed the music of Bohemia. He also continued to compose great new works, which were enthusiastically received.

Another terrible tragedy in his life—deafness—did not stop his work. Smetana spent five years (in total deafness) composing his masterpiece, the six national tone poems collectively entitled *My Country*. It remains today one of his most performed works. One of those tone poems, *The Moldau*, gives a magnificent picture of the beautiful river that brought life to his land.

I dare say that Czech music would not have thrived without this man's commitment to his land. Thousands of Czechs studied in his institutions, and he encouraged local composers to write music in the flavor of their cherished country. His work almost singlehandedly paved the way for talented Czechs such as Antonin Dvořák (1841–1904), Joseph Suk (1874–1935), Leos Janacek (1854–1928), and Bohuslav Martinu (1890–1959).

Smetana died in Prague in 1884 after many years of faithful service to his country. He remains so loved by his people that in 1924—the centenary of Smetana's birth—every single village in the new republic of Czechoslovakia took part in a grandiose celebration.

Like Nehemiah after rebuilding Jerusalem, perhaps Smetana, too, could pray, "Remember me for this also, O my God, and show mercy to me according to your great love" (Neh. 13:22).

Has it been too long since love of your country inspired you to some act of service or some act of thanksgiving—even to an act of prayer? When was the last time you thanked God for your country or prayed for its leaders? Give it some thought today. Give it some time this week.

Lord, I ask You for a greater love of my wonderful country and a grateful heart for all that it means to me. Please forgive me when I take my country and my heritage for granted. Help me to appreciate the freedoms and privileges with which You have blessed me and my fellow citizens.

For this reason a man will leave his father and mother and be united to his wife, and they will become one flesh.
—Genesis 2:24

ROBERT SCHUMANN (1810–1856) AND CLARA WIECK SCHUMANN (1819–1896)

Inspired by Love Fulfilled

Young Robert Schumann had thought this day would never come. He had loved Clara Wieck for five years, and for most of that time her father had forbidden them to see each other. Mr. Wieck had set his heart on a concert career for his pianist daughter, and this young, tempestuous composer had not been part of the plan.

But this love would not die. Whenever possible they had exchanged love letters. Robert wrote, "Someday my turn will come, then you will see how much I love you." Clara replied, "I say to you again that my love knows no bounds."

After Clara had come of age and her father still refused their marriage, Schumann had gone to court. After hearing Mr. Wieck rant and rave through months of an ugly trial, the judges sided with the young couple.

At long last, in a country church in Schoenfeld, Robert and Clara were married on September 12, 1840. That evening, Clara wrote in her diary, "This has been the loveliest and most important day of my life. Now begins a new existence, a beautiful life, a life wrapped up in him whom I love more than myself and everything else."

Robert's jubilation was immediately channeled into creative energy. In the first year of their marriage, he virtually exploded with masterpiece after masterpiece; he wrote more than one hundred beautiful songs and three of the greatest

song cycles ever composed: *Liederkreis* ("Song Cycle," Op. 39), *Frauenliebe und Leben* ("Woman's Love and Life," Op. 42), and *Dichterliebe* ("Poet's Love," Op. 48).

Within a few years of their marriage, Robert had composed symphonies, chamber music, and piano works that placed his name among those of the world's finest composers. Many of these works were directly inspired by—and performed by—his brilliant wife, Clara. One can easily visualize her husband beaming while she premiered his *Piano Concerto* with the Gewandhaus Orchestra or performed his *Piano Quintet* with friends in their own house.

Clara was not only a world-class pianist and a composer in her own right but also a dedicated mother (of eight children, five of whom survived) and an encouraging wife. She once told Robert, "No one alive is as gifted as you. My growing love and admiration for you can hardly keep pace with each other."

I am inspired by this couple who allowed their love for each other to fuel their talents, reminiscent of Shakespeare's line, "If music be the food of love, play on"—but I would transpose a few words: "If love be the food of music, love on."

The Scriptures clearly call us to a life of fidelity. And in a good marriage that faithful love can bring out the very best in both spouses. Do you try to draw out the gifts of your mate, allowing him or her to serve others and enjoy life to the full?

Take a lesson from Robert and Clara, whose love produced works that have inspired millions of music lovers.

Lord, I thank You for my spouse and for the love You have placed between us. Help me to find new ways to encourage my loved one. Help me to overlook my mate's faults and to focus on and praise my partner's many virtues. Give us more of Your love every day, and help our love to be an inspiration to others as well.

Keep yourselves in God's love as you wait for the mercy of our Lord Jesus Christ to bring you to eternal life.
—Jude 21

Charles Wesley (1707–1788)

Inspired by the Love of God

It was Charles's birthday—though not a day for public celebration, as this was not a natural birthday but a spiritual one. Just one year before, Charles Wesley—already an ordained clergyman and experienced missionary—had been convicted by the Holy Spirit and had committed his life to Christ. Three days later his older brother John—with similar "religious" credentials—had experienced a similar conversion in a Moravian mission on Aldersgate Street in London.

In May 1738 both men had been transformed—inspired to preach to anyone who would listen to the Good News of salvation by faith in Christ.

Now Charles pondered the events of the last year. He and John had made enemies, though God had been faithful through every trial. Did Charles contemplate the future of his ministry? Would he have blanched to know of the persecution to come? He and John would be prohibited from church pulpits and subsequently preach in open fields. Even then they would be hounded from town to town.

The Wesleys' "Methodist" converts would be threatened with death, their businesses destroyed, and their homes burned. He and his brother would be universally denounced. Yet Charles would continue to praise God through it all, writing more than six thousand hymns for followers to sing.

On this spiritual birthday, Charles turned to his favorite avocation: hymnwriting. In this day's song, would he relive the hurdles of the previous year? Would he worry about the future? Or would the new hymn reflect his burning love for God? Taking his pen in hand, Charles filled the page with the joy that filled his soul:

O for a thousand tongues to sing
My great Redeemer's praise,
The glories of my God and King,
The triumphs of his grace.

There are six verses to this birthday song. You may be familiar with them all. I can hardly imagine a more accurate word picture of joy than Wesley's last verse:

Hear Him, ye deaf; His praise, ye dumb;
Your loosened tongues employ;
Ye blind behold your Savior come;
And leap, ye lame, for joy.

What was the secret of Charles Wesley's steadfast, sustaining joy? You can see it in the title of a song he'd written earlier in that first year of his Christian walk: "Jesus, Lover of My Soul." When enemies persecuted him, when friends disappointed him, Wesley drew strength and inspiration from a higher relationship. Charles was sustained by the only love large enough to conquer a man's heart and fill it with praise.

Today, even if things go against you, try praising God. Praise Him for who He is, for what He has done for all of us, for the future He holds for you. Praise Him as the lover of your soul.

Lord, my love is but a reflection of Your greater love. Fill me with a fresh sense of Your passionate love for me. And inspire me to serve You and praise You as if I had a thousand tongues.

For we are God's workmanship, created in Christ Jesus to do good works, which God prepared in advance for us to do.
—Ephesians 2:10

George Frédéric Handel (1685–1759)

Inspired!

In 1741, George Frédéric Handel was genuinely discouraged. His health was failing, audiences had deserted him, and he was deeply in debt. Seeing no hope for the future, his music, or his life, he was ready to retire in disgrace.

It seems that God had other plans for Handel. Two challenges almost simultaneously set before him changed his life and the map of the musical world. From a Dublin charity, he received a commission to compose a piece of music for a benefit concert. From Charles Jennings, a wealthy friend, he received a libretto based exclusively on Bible texts.

With that libretto in hand, Handel went into a feverish work mode. For three weeks, beginning on August 22, he confined himself to his small house on Brook Street in London. From early morning into the night, he rarely left his music paper, ink, and pens. A friend who visited at that time reported having seen Handel weeping with intense emotion. Later, as Handel related the compositional experience, he quoted St. Paul's words: "Whether I was in the body or out of my body when I wrote it, I know not."

At one point a servant came into Handel's room to deliver a tray of food. He reported having seen a wild expression in his employer's eyes; a weeping Handel refused the food and exclaimed, "I did think I did see all Heaven before me, and the great God Himself." He had just completed what has

become the most-performed choral movement in history, the "Hallelujah Chorus."

After six days of this incredibly concentrated work, Handel had completed Part 1. Part 2 took him nine days, and Part 3 another six. In two more days—to complete the orchestration—the masterpiece called the *Messiah* was finished. In the unbelievably brief span of twenty-four days, Handel had filled two hundred sixty pages of manuscript.

One of Handel's many biographers, Sir Newman Flower, gave this summation: "Considering the immensity of the work, and the short time involved, it will remain, perhaps forever, the greatest feat in the whole history of music composition."

And musicologist Robert Myers has stated that the music and its powerful message "has probably done more to convince thousands of mankind that there is a God about us than all the theological works ever written."

Handel's own aspirations for this masterpiece were revealed after the first London performance of *Messiah*. When the concert ended, Lord Kinnoul congratulated Handel on the superb "entertainment." Handel's reply? "My lord, I should be sorry if I only entertain them; I wish to make them better."

With such a spiritual purpose, it is no surprise that the Lord blessed this talented man with a special grace to compose such a powerful piece.

In the midst of a depression, did Handel set out to write the most celebrated choral music of all time? Probably not. But Handel was a man listening to the voice of God. Struck with the power of the words of Scripture, he opened himself to the Holy Spirit and let the Spirit work through him to produce what can be described as a *wonder*.

Although you and I might not produce the world's next choral *Messiah*, each of us can be ever listening to the voice of God—as He speaks through the Scriptures, through opportunities set before us, through friends, directly to our spirits. And we, too, can produce masterpieces. As you step out in faith, remember God's promise:

"Whether you turn to the right or to the left, your ears will hear a voice behind you, saying, 'This is the way; walk in it'" (Isa. 30:21).

Lord, how wonderful to think that You can lead me and inspire me! Father, help me to always seek You in my work and to listen to Your Spirit's word to me. And in everything, remind me to give You all the credit, all the glory. Hallelujah!

For Further Reading

The following is a short bibliography for those who wish to find additional information about the composers mentioned in *Spiritual Moments with the Great Composers*:

Thomas Arne

Cummings, William Hayman. *Dr. Arne and Rule Britannia*. London: Novello and Company, 1912.

Johann Sebastian Bach

Geiringer, Karl. *Johann Sebastian Bach—The Culmination of an Era*. New York: Oxford University Press, 1966.

Schweitzer, Albert. *J. S. Bach*, trans. Ernest Newman. Boston: Humphries, 1964.

Spitta, Philipp. *Johann Sebastian Bach, His Work and Influence on the Music of Germany*, trans. Clara Bell and J. A. Fuller-Maitland. New York: Dover, 1951.

Béla Bartók

Lesznai, Lajos. *Bartók*, trans. Percy M. Young. New York: Octagon, 1973.

Stevens, Halsey. *The Life and Music of Béla Bartók*, rev. ed. New York: Oxford University Press, 1964.

Ludwig van Beethoven

Marek, George. *Beethoven: Biography of a Genius*. New York: Funk & Wagnalls Company, 1969.

Sullivan, J. W. N. *Beethoven: His Spiritual Development*. New York: New American Library, Mentor Books, 1954.

Thayer, Alexander Wheelock. *The Life of Beethoven*, rev. and ed. Elliott Forbes. Princeton, N.J.: Princeton University Press, 1964.

Hector Berlioz

Barzun, Jacques. *Berlioz and the Romantic Century*, 3rd ed. New York: Columbia University Press, 1969.

Turner, Walter J. *Berlioz, the Man and His Work*. New York: Vienna House, 1974.

Leonard Bernstein

Briggs, John. *Leonard Bernstein, the Man, His Work, and His World*. Cleveland: World Publishing Company, 1961.

Johannes Brahms

Evans, Edwin. *Handbook to the Works of Johannes Brahms*. New York: Lenox Hill, 1970.

Geiringer, Karl. *Brahms, His Life and Work*, trans. H. B. Weiner and Bernard Miall, 2nd ed., rev. and enl. London: Allen & Unwin, 1963.

Latham, Peter. *Brahms*. New York: Collier, 1962.

Pablo Casals

Kirk, H. L. *Pablo Casals*. New York: Holt, Rinehart, and Winston, 1974.

Pier Franceso Cavalli

Glover, Jane. *Cavalli*. New York: St. Martin's Press, 1978.

Frédéric Chopin

Chissell, Joan. *Chopin*. London: Faber & Faber, 1965.

Hedley, Arthur. *Chopin*, ed. and rev. Maurice J. E. Brown. London: J. M. Dent, 1974.

Walker, Ian, ed. *The Chopin Companion, Profiles of the Man and the Musician*. New York: Norton, 1973.

Carl Czerny

Dreetz, Albert. *Czerny and Beethoven*. Leipzig: Kistner and Company, 1932.

Antonin Dvořák

Clapham, John. *Antonin Dvořák*. London: St. Martin's 1966.

Hughes, Gervase. *Dvořák: His Life and Music*. New York: Dodd, Mead, 1967.

Robertson, Alec. *Dvořák*. New York: Collier, 1962.

Edvard Grieg

Horton, John. *Grieg*. London: J. M. Dent, 1974.

Johansen, David Monrad. *Edvard Grieg*, trans. Madge Robertson. Princeton, N. J.: Princeton University Press, 1938.

George Frédéric Handel

Abraham, Gerald. *Handel: A Symposium*. London: Oxford University Press, 1954.

Lang, Paul Henry. *George Frédéric Handel*. New York: Norton, 1966.

Young, Percy M. *Handel*, rev. ed. New York: Farrar, Straus & Giroux, 1965.

Franz Joseph Haydn

Geiringer, Karl, in collaboration with Irene Geiringer. *Haydn: A Creative Life in Music*, 2nd ed., rev. and enl. Berkeley, Calif.: University of California Press, 1968.

Hughes, Rosemary. *Haydn*. New York: Collier, 1962.

Arthur Honegger

Delannoy, Marcel Francois Georges. *Honegger*. Paris: P. Horay, 1953.

Charles Ives

Cowell, Henry, and Sydney Cowell. *Charles Ives and His Music*. New York: Oxford University Press, 1955.

Perry, Rosalie S. *Charles Ives and the American Mind*. Kent, Ohio: Kent State University Press, 1974.

Zoltán Kodály

Eosze, Laszlo. *Zoltán Kodály, His Life and Work*. Boston: Crescendo Publications, 1962.

Ruggiero Leoncavallo

Von Keler, Theodore Maximilian. *I Pagliacci*. Girald: Haldeman-Julius Company, 1923.

Franz Liszt

Sitwell, Sacheverell. *Liszt*. New York: Dover, 1967.

Walker, Alan. *Franz Liszt, the Man and His Music*. New York: Taplinger, 1970.

Felix Mendelssohn

Jacob, Heinrich E. *Felix Mendelssohn and His Times*, trans. Richard Weston and Clara Weston. Westport, Conn.: Greenwood Press, 1973.

Radcliffe, Philip. *Mendelssohn*, rev. ed. New York: Collier, 1967.

Werner, Eric. *Mendelssohn: A New Image of the Composer and His Age*. trans. Dika Newlin. New York: Free Press, 1963.

Wolfgang Amadeus Mozart

Einstein, Alfred. *Mozart: His Character, His Work*, trans. Arthur Mendel and Nathan Broder. New York: Oxford University Press, 1945.

Landon, H. C. Robbins, ed. *The Mozart Companion*. London: Oxford University Press, 1956.

Turner, Walter J. *Mozart: The Man and His Works*, rev. and ed. Christopher Raeburn. New York: Barnes & Noble, 1966.

Modest Mussorgsky

Calvocoressi, M. D. *Mussorgsky*, completed and rev. G. Abraham. London: J. M. Dent, 1974.

Jacques Offenbach

Hughes, George. *Composers of Operetta*. London: Novello and Company, 1962.

Nicholas Rimsky-Korsakov

Beaumont, Cyril William. *Scheherazade*. London: C. W. Beaumont, 1919.

Arnold Schoenberg

Payne, Anthony. *Schoenberg*. New York: Oxford University Press, 1968.

Reich, Willi. *Schoenberg, A Critical Biography*, trans. Leo Black. New York: Praeger, 1972.

Franz Schubert

Abraham, Gerald, ed. *The Music of Schubert*. New York: Norton, 1947.

Brown, Maurice J. E. *Schubert: A Critical Biography*. London: Macmillan, 1958.

Hutchings, Arthur. *Schubert*, rev. ed. New York: Octagon, 1973.

Clara Schumann

Harding, Bertita. *Concerto, the Story of Clara Schumann*. London: G. G. Harrap 1962.

Robert Schumann

Abraham, Gerald, ed. *Schumann: A Symposium*. New York: Oxford University Press, 1952.

Chissell, Joan. *Schumann*, rev. ed. New York: Collier, 1967.

Dmitri Shostakovich

Martinov, Ivan Ivanovich. *Dmitri Shostakovich, the Man and His Work*. New York: Greenwood Press, 1969.

Bedřich Smetana

Clapham, John. *Smetana*. New York: Octagon, 1972.

Large, Brian. *Smetana*. New York: Praeger, 1971.

Igor Stravinsky

Strobel, Heinrich. *Stravinsky: Classic Humanist*, trans. Hans Rosenwald. New York: Da Capo Press, 1973.

Vlad, Roman. *Stravinsky*, trans. Frederick Fuller and Ann Fuller, 2nd ed. New York: Oxford University Press, 1967.

White, Eric Walter. *Stravinsky: The Composer and His Works*. Berkeley, Calif.: University of California Press, 1966.

Peter Illych Tchaikovsky

Abraham, Gerald, ed. *Tchaikovsky: A Symposium*. London: Drummond, 1946.

Evans, Edwin. *Tchaikovsky*, rev. ed. New York: Farrar, Straus & Giroux, 1966.

Hanson, Laurence, and Elisabeth Hanson. *Tchaikovsky: The Man Behind the Music*. New York: Dodd, Mead, 1966.

Giuseppe Verdi

Gatti, Carlo. *Verdi: The Man and His Music*, trans. Elisabeth Abbott. New York: Putnam's, 1955.

Toe, Francis. *Giuseppe Verdi: His Life and Works*. New York: Random House, 1946.

Walker, Frank. *The Man Verdi*. New York: Knopf, 1962.

Richard Wagner

Gutman, Robert W. *Richard Wagner: The Man, His Mind and His Music*. New York: Harcourt Brace Jovanovich, 1968.

Newman, Ernest. *The Life of Richard Wagner*. New York: Knopf, 1949.

Books About Composers

Brockway, W. and H. Weinstock. *Men of Music*. New York: Simon and Schuster, 1958.

Ewen, David. *The World of Great Composers*. Englewood Cliffs, NJ: Prentice-Hall, 1962.

Grammand, P. The Harmony Illustrated Encyclopedia of Classical Music. New York: Harmony Books, 1988.

Kavanaugh, Patrick. *The Spiritual Lives of Great Composers*. Nashville, TN: Sparrow Press, 1992.

Slonimsky, Nicolas. Baker's Biographical Dictionary of Musicians, 8th ed. New York: G. Schirmer, 1991.

Thompson, O. *International Cyclopedia of Music and Musicians*. New York: Dodd, Mead, 1975.

Westrup, J., ed. The Master Musicians Series. London: J. M. Dent, 1954.

Books About Hymnwriters

Barrows, Cliff. *Crusade Hymn Stories*. Chicago: Hope Publishing Company, 1967.

Davies, James P. *Sing with Understanding*. Chicago: Covenant Press, 1966.

Erickson, J. Irving. *Twice-Born Hymns*. Chicago: Covenant Press, 1976.

Thompson, Ronald W. *Who's Who of Hymn Writers*. London: Epworth Press, 1967.

For information on the Christian Performing Artists' Fellowship, or their annual performing arts festival, write or call: CPAF, 10523 Main Street, Suite 31, Fairfax, Virginia 22030 (703) 385-CPAF